50 Hikes in Southern Maine

Day Hikes and Walks in Southwestern,
Central, and Coastal Maine

John Gibson

Photographs by the author

Backcountry Publications
Woodstock, Vermont

An Invitation to the Reader

Over time trails can be rerouted and signs and landmarks altered. If you find that changes have occurred on the routes described in this book, please let us know so that corrections may be made in future editions. The author and publisher also welcome other comments and suggestions. Address all correspondence to:

Editor
Fifty Hikes™ Series
Backcountry Publications
PO Box 175
Woodstock, Vermont 05091-0175

Library of Congress Cataloging-in-Publication Data

Gibson, John, 1940–

    Fifty hikes in southern Maine: day hikes and walks in southwestern, central, and coastal Maine/John Gibson; photographs by the author.
    p. cm.—(Fifty hikes series)
  "A fifty hikes guide."
  ISBN 0-88150-128-X:
    1. Hiking—Maine—Guide-books. 2. Maine—Description and travel—1981– —Guide-books. I. Title. II. Title: 50 hikes in southern Maine. III. Series.
GV199.42.M2G54 1989
917.41—dc19   89-6501
                                               CIP

Published by Backcountry Publications,
a division of The Countryman Press, Inc.,
PO Box 175, Woodstock, Vermont 05091-0175.

Printed in the United States of America
Typesetting by Corinne Arndt Girouard
Series design by Wladislaw Finne
Trail overlays by Richard Widhu

Cover photograph by the author.
Photographs on page 27 and 172 by Russell D. Butcher.
Photographs on page 67, 71, 76, and 190 by Cloe Caputo.
All other photographs by the author.

Portions of this book originally appeared in *Fifty Hikes in Maine* by John Gibson (1976, 1983) and *Fifty More Hikes in Maine* by Cloe Catlett (1980), both published by Backcountry Publications.

This book is dedicated to all those people who have, on so many occasions, worked to protect the trails and hills of Maine.

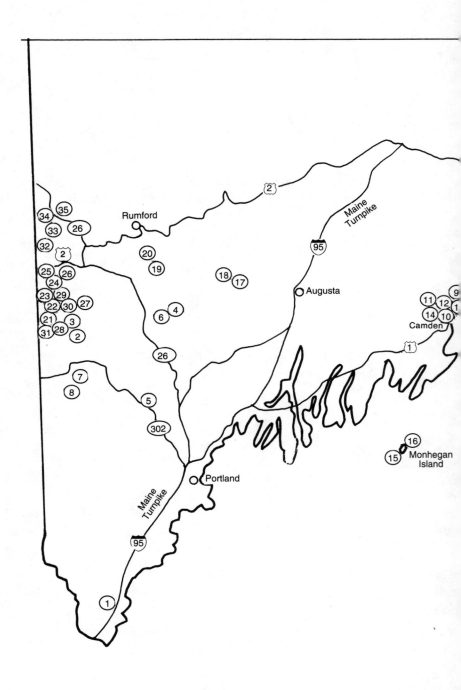

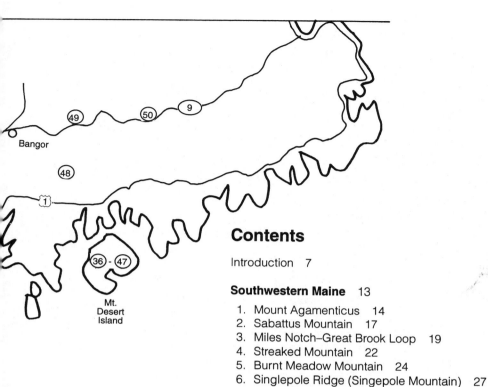

Bangor

Mt.
Desert
Island

Contents

Introduction

In the years since my first book in this series, *Fifty Hikes in Maine*, appeared, the hiking boom has come and gone and, now, come again. Many people have discovered there are few things so satisfying as a good tramp in the Maine woods. This book, updated and with new material, is dedicated to those persons who made such a success of the earlier volume, and who today want a current guide to some of the best trails in Maine.

Readers will note that this edition covers all of southern, central, and coastal Maine. (A companion volume, *Fifty Hikes in Northern Maine*, by Cloe Caputo, describes trails in the northern half of the state.) Hikes are organized into major regions, such as the Mahoosucs, Evans Notch, Mount Desert, and the Camden Hills. Full travel instructions accompany each hike description so that even a novice hiker, unfamiliar with the Maine countryside, can find and enjoy the excursions described here. Regardless of the kind of hiking you enjoy, you are likely to find it in this book. In the case of the hikes carried over from earlier editions, the trails have been rewalked and directions updated to reflect changes in conditions.

Persons who love the outdoors and care for the Maine woods know that, since *Fifty Hikes in Maine* debuted, the Maine backcountry has changed. When that book was prepared in 1974–75, the backcountry was tranquil, and the traditional industries of logging and farming followed time-honored practices. Today, rural Maine is besieged by unprecedented pressure for development. Out-of-state land companies have bought large tracts of Maine land and are selling plots big enough to escape environmental controls. The paper companies have recently put very large holdings on the auction block, creating the possibility that thousands of acres of woodlands will become "vacation home" disasters. Many sections of coastal Maine threaten to go under the developer's bulldozer, becoming condominium settlements or worse. The picture is not an encouraging one.

Users of this book who are concerned that the trails of Maine remain wild and free in their natural state *must* act. As you walk the routes described herein, think about what it will mean if Maine woods and farmlands continue to disappear at the present alarming rate. Whether you're a hiker, camper, hunter, fisherman, or just someone who loves to wander in the woods and hills, we *all* have a stake in opposing this frightening assault on the Maine backcountry. Write your newspaper editor, your state senator and state representative, your governor, and your congressional representatives. Support the conservation organizations that are fighting the uphill battle to regulate explosive and exploitive development in Maine (see "Resources" at end of introduction). Refuse to patronize businesses who throw their lot in with irresponsible developers. In short, we must act *now* to keep Maine woods and farmlands open to the hikers and sportspersons of tomorrow.

Despite new developmental realities,

much of Maine still lies in woodlands and hill country of unusual beauty. Hiking those hills remains one of the more refreshing, energizing experiences left to each of us for no greater cost than the effort of walking. The trail descriptions in these pages will point you in the right direction and bring you home again. Walk softly in the woods of Maine, and leave no trace of your passing. The next generation will thank you.

Trails

The trails described in *50 Hikes in Southern Maine* range from easy, well-defined paths along tote roads to demanding, tough-to-follow routes over rock faces, streambeds, and through brushy, rough terrain. The maps and descriptions in the book make it pretty hard to get lost, and trail commentary warns of any noticeable problems along the way. Trail descriptions were revised and current at time of publication, but weathering, blowdowns, and trail relocation may change the direction of a given route at any time. Most trails are "blazed" with paint markers, but some have not been marked recently, or their blazes have weathered bare. One should always carry a compass when hiking anywhere in Maine, even in settled areas. US Geological Survey and other maps are useful, although not essential, supplements to the maps in

this book. (See "Directions and Maps" below.) Beware of Maine's unpredictable climate. Should inclement weather overtake you on the higher peaks, don't continue upward, but always *head down* for safety.

Clothing and Boots

Hiking clothing has always been a matter of one's own eccentric tastes. Major design improvements have made hiking wear a lot more comfortable and functional in the last several years.

Basically, shorts and cotton-synthetic shirts are suitable outerwear for summer. Long pants and a wool shirt, sweater, and wind shell are appropriate for cooler weather. For day hikes, a lightweight poncho or rain jacket of coated nylon or Gore-Tex, a hat, a down vest, and an extra pair of socks are all worthy items in your pack. Gloves are worth carrying in spring and fall.

Always overestimate your clothing needs. Temperatures on high summits are frequently much cooler than those at the roadside. Wind-chill can leave you cold and shivering even on sunny days when temperature would normally be comfortable. Prepare accordingly.

Footwear, like clothing, remains a matter of individual preference. Any time a bunch of hikers get together, heated discussions of what is "best" for your feet will likely follow. Maine trails are usually rough, and sneakers and street shoes are out of the question. Vibram-soled boots are preferable, with sturdy, 6 inch uppers. There are many good brands on the market, but they are no longer cheap. A good pair of hiking boots, such as those made by Fabiano, Galiber, Lowa, Asolo, or Vasque, costs from $95 to $200. There are no inexpensive alternatives, for bargain basement boots tend to fall apart on the trail,

possibly failing you at a dangerous moment. Jogging shoes and the new boots made with synthetic cloth uppers should be avoided. A quality hiking boot will last many years, so we're talking about an investment of only a few dollars for each season's use. Not bad, when you think of it that way.

Backpacks and Tents

Backpacks have undergone major changes recently. Hikers are getting away from the enormous, unwieldly frame packs that were sold everywhere in the 70s. Back-hugging soft packs, which carry well and move *with* you, are now widely available. A good small- to medium-sized rucksack is all you'll need for most day trips in Maine. Larger rucksacks for overnighters and extended trips are made by Kelty, Berghaus, Karrimor, North Face, L.L. Bean, REI, Lowe, and Camp Trails. Frame packs are a poor choice for the Maine backcountry because they tend to catch on every low-hanging branch or bush you pass.

A tent is worth its weight in reliable shelter for longer trips in the Maine mountains. The heavy canvas tentage of 10 years ago has been replaced by super lightweight portable shelters weighing only 4 or 5 pounds. Sleeping bags are also more compact and lighter. If you choose your equipment carefully, you should be able to get away for several days in the mountains with no more than 30 pounds on your back.

Cooking

If you're hiking for more than a day, carry your own stove. Chopping down trees and destroying vegetation to build a campfire is not only foolish, it's often illegal. There are many excellent

backpacking stoves, tiny and light-weight, which operate on white gasoline or butane. Plan meals that lend themselves to one-pot preparation. Your mountaineering shop has freeze-dried foods to supplement the quick meals available in your supermarket.

Drinking Water

Stream pollution is still rare in Maine, but especially near settled areas, it's wise to boil or disinfect your water—or carry in your own safe water. Streams flowing in fields where there are cattle are particularly suspect. Much has been written in the way of warnings about *giardia* recently, too. This is a naturally occurring parasite, frequently transmitted by beavers, as well as humans, that may occasionally be found in mountain streams and ponds. It is a most unpleasant affliction, as the parasitic cysts fasten themselves to the stomach lining and cause nausea, cramps, diarrhea, and transient feverish symptoms. It would, however, take an awful lot of heavily infested water passing through your body to create the likelihood of a really bad case of *giardia*. Still, it's wisest to get your water from a spring, or if you must use stream water, choose a fast-moving stream and then boil, disinfect, or filter it. Better still, fill your water bottle back home or at a known safe water site whenever possible.

Directions and Maps

Trail descriptions and maps in this book are oriented to *true* north, which is about 18 to 20 degrees *right* of magnetic north on your compass. For easy reference, always carry this book or a photocopy of the hike with you as you walk. Each hike description lists the total distance you will walk from start to finish, from roadside to summit and return. Approximate vertical rise is also listed, giving you some idea of the total amount of climbing you'll be doing, as some trails rise and descend several times before greatest elevation is reached. The suggested hiking time for each route is based on comfortable walking time, not a mad dash. There are many summits on which you'll want to linger, enjoying the view and the Maine air.

The maps in this book have been prepared on backgrounds taken from United States Geological Survey (USGS) maps. The hikes described were drawn in, together with important trailside features (see key at end of introduction), after the text had been prepared and thus reflect trail routes and the latest information available at the time of publication. The use of USGS maps as background is designed to show contours and generally give the hiker a feel for the land he or she will be hiking.

You will not need maps other than those in this book to make the hikes, but I have listed maps at the beginning of each hike that can provide additional information on geographical features—and on the views you will see from the mountaintops. Most of those listed are USGS maps, which can be obtained at many book, sports, and hardware stores throughout Maine, or directly from the USGS. For those hikes using sections of the Appalachian Trail, the maps published by the Maine Appalachian Trail Club (MATC) are also useful. In addition, the Appalachian Mountain Club's maps cover sections of the Mahoosuc Range in Maine, the Rangeley region, Acadian National Park, and Baxter State Park. For ordering addresses, see the end of this section.

A word of caution is in order regarding USGS maps. For much of Maine, only the older, less-detailed 15-minute series maps are available. Maps in this series, made in the 1930s or earlier, may be seriously out of date. The topography is unchanged, but long-vanished houses, fire towers, roads, railroads, and trails may still be shown, while new roads and trails do not appear. Fortunately, many of the hikes in this book are in areas of which the newer, more-detailed 7½-minute series maps are available. The 7½-minute series, prepared in the 1960s, is generally accurate, although an occasional new forest service road or other recent man-made feature may be missing.

Resources

For further information about hiking opportunities in Maine and the conservation of Maine's wilderness, you may wish to write or call one or more of the following organizations:

United States Geological Survey
Box 25286, Denver Federal Center
Denver, CO 80225
(303-236-7477)

Maine Appalachian Trail Club
Box 283
Augusta, ME 04330

Appalachian Mountain Club
5 Joy Street
Boston, MA 02108
(617-523-0636)

Maine Audubon Society
188 US Route 1
Falmouth, ME 04105
(207-781-2330)

Sportsman's Alliance of Maine
Box 2783
Augusta, ME 04330

New England Sierra Club
5 Joy Street
Boston, MA 02108

Maine Coast Heritage Trust
167 Park Row
Brunswick, ME 04011
(207-729-7366)

Natural Resources Council of Maine
271 State Street
Augusta, ME 04330
(207-622-3101)

The Nature Conservancy
Box 338
122 Main Street
Topsham, ME 04086
(207-729-5181)

Key to Map Symbols

——— main trail

— — — side trail

A Appalachian Trail

Δ campground

lookout

Ⓟ parking

ⅅ shelter

brook

o o oo stone wall

—·—· dirt road

gate

Southwestern Maine

1

Mount Agamenticus

Distance (round trip): 1 mile
Hiking time: 40 minutes
Vertical rise: 350 feet
Map: USGS 7½' York Harbor

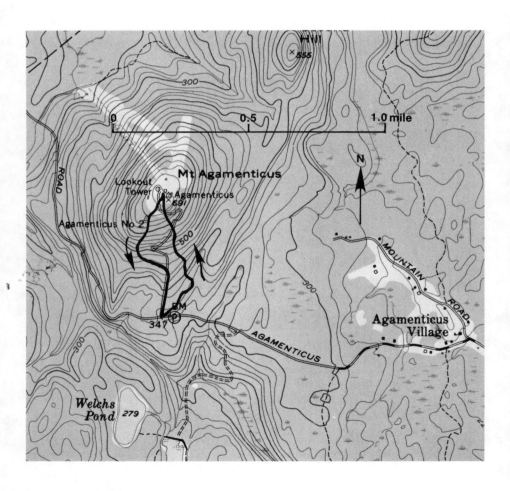

Mount Agamenticus, in exchange for an easy, brief hike, offers superb views. It is no more than a ledgy hummock on the coastal map which you can scramble up in short order, but the perspective from the summit belies its elevation. A good destination for some light afternoon tramping in spring and autumn, Agamenticus is easily accessible from Boston and Portland.

The mountain may be reached either from the Maine Turnpike (I-95) or from US 1 in the Cape Neddick section of York. If you travel via I-95, take the York exit and cross to the west side of the highway. Turn right or north on Chase's Pond Road, which parallels the interstate. Follow this route approximately 3 miles northward to a junction with Mountain Road, on which you continue in a more westerly direction. If you approach the mountain from US 1, turn west in Cape Neddick on Mountain Road (sometimes called Agamenticus Road) and drive westward, intersecting Chase's Pond Road in 1.3 miles. From this junction, drive west another 2.7 miles, where the paved road ends abruptly. Park your car here at the foot of the summit road.

The path to the summit departs through the trees on an old woods road by the gravel parking area. The way leads gradually upward through tall pines and fir, coming shortly to a junction. Keep left here, rising more briskly through denser growth and to the northwest through a crumbling stone wall. The path soon emerges in a clearing just to the right side of the mountain road where the power line crosses. Keep to the right and under the power line as it climbs northward and away from the road up a series of granite ledges. Unmarked here, the route is easily followed over the rock. Thin stands of red oak, yellow pine, and scattered, immature birch line both sides of the path's corridor.

Climbing steadily, the way shortly crosses the road (watch for speeding cars) and continues up through a gully bordered by scrub oak. Just below the summit road, the path bends slightly to the left, crosses a grassy spot, and emerges on the left side of the road opposite a telephone relay tower. Follow the road straight to the fire tower and to the left of the main summit buildings, which are not open to the public.

Agamenticus's summit bears the fallen-down remains of a ski operation. Rusty stanchions, once active in pulling skiers up the north side of the mountain, now stand alone, looking like lost, old men. No matter, climb the lookout tower and enjoy the fine, 360-degree view. If the tower observer is in, as she may be in summer, you might be invited to climb into the cabin and share the perspective, the forest service radio crackling in the background.

To the north-northwest are the low hills of Sanford and Ossipee Hill in Waterboro. On exceptionally fine days (some of the best of which come in winter), you may be able to see Mount Washington and other peaks in New Hampshire's Presidential Range. York Village lies southeast of your lookout, with Kittery and Portsmouth further down the coast and more around to the south. East and northeast, you'll have excellent views up the southern Maine coast and, of course, out toward the Atlantic. A fair variety of bird life may be seen from the tower and in the woods around the summit. One afternoon, I spent nearly an hour watching a turkey vulture ride the thermals about a half mile to the west, looking for dinner.

To head down, go back to the point where you emerged onto the road by the telephone relay disks, and turn right

Northward from Mount Agamenticus

entering the woods further west by a bent tree. Here, the path drops slowly to the southwest and south through evergreens and mixed growth. The grade becomes steeper and, in about ¼ mile, you come to a "T" with an old tote road. Bear left here, walking south and east, and you will soon emerge on the paved mountain road. Simply follow it downhill to your starting point.

Sabattus Mountain

Distance (round trip): 1 mile
Hiking time: 40 minutes
Vertical rise: 500 feet
Map: USGS 7½' North Waterford

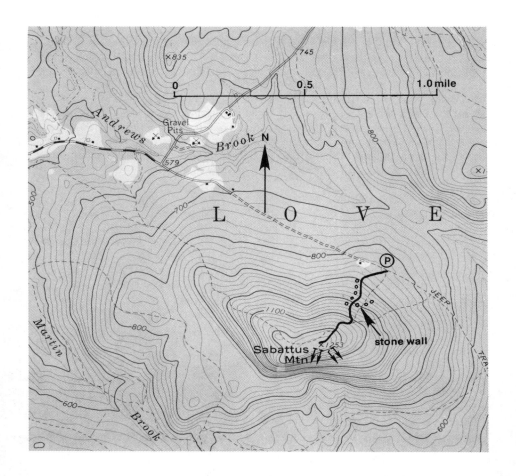

Good things sometimes come in small packages—and that goes for mountains too. Sabattus (elevation 1280 feet) is short work, but it offers one of the finest mountain panoramas I know. And, you needn't go all that far north in the Pine Tree State to enjoy the view.

Getting to the trailhead is simple. From the intersection of ME 5 and ME 5A in Center Lovell, head north on ME 5, turning right onto a paved road after 0.7 mile. At 1.5 miles from ME 5, a gravel road forks right, uphill. Turn here, and proceed about 0.3 mile to a parking area on the left, just past the Willoby place.

The trail leaves opposite the parking area and is marked by a weathered sign next to a great, old pine. You walk west and southwest through dense, tall pines, beech, and an occasional maple. A fine mossy stone wall is quickly reached, and you turn sharply toward the south, walking parallel to the old wall.

At ¼ mile, you leave the evergreen groves, cross another stone wall, and head south and southeast through young second-growth hardwoods. Shortly, you ascend steeply out of this cut-over area, heading up the lower peak.

The trail levels off momentarily, then recommences climbing to a broad, ledgy area topped by a stark, weathered pine. Continue over this rise, through a slump, and climb directly to the main summit, former site of the now-dismantled fire tower.

The great cliffs which form the southwest flanks of Sabattus are immediately below you. The views range splendidly from southeast to northwest. The imposing mass of Pleasant Mountain in Bridgton is nearly due south over Kezar Pond. More to the right, you can see into North Conway, where the drumlin-shaped mass that holds Cathedral and White Horse ledges is visible. To the west, beyond Kezar Lake, stretch the Presidentials, Robbins Ridge above Kearsarge, and the Carter-Moriah Range. Sharply northwest are the mountains below and around Evans Notch. It's truly a fine sight, and a perch you'll not quickly abandon. Eminently worth some camera work on a clear day before you make the quick descent to your car.

South from Sabattus Mountain

Miles Notch–Great Brook Loop

Distance (around loop): 10¾ miles
Hiking time: 6½ hours
Vertical rise: 1800 feet
Map: USGS 7½' Speckled Mountain

A hike into Miles Notch and over the adjoining summits to the west combines a long woods walk with some excellent ridge-running. The Miles Notch–Red Rock route traverses three 2000-foot mountains due east of Evans Notch and northeast of Speckled Mountain. The return along Great Brook is refreshing in summer, and the ridge walk over Elizabeth, Red Rock, and Butters Mountains provides fine views south to Kezar Lake and north toward Caribou Mountain.

The V-shaped route up the notch, over the summits, and back down from the west will occupy a full day's hiking, and extra food and clothing should be packed along accordingly.

Although not as remote from traveled roads as some climbs in this book, the Miles Notch area is mountainous, deep-woods country, and a guide to the local terrain (USGS 7½' Speckled Mountain quadrangle) plus a compass should be included in your rucksack.

The trail may be approached from the north or south on ME 5. Turn west off ME 5 in North Lovell by the Evergreen Valley sign. Follow this road into Evergreen Valley for exactly 1.8 miles to where a narrow, paved road departs to the right at a very sharp angle. Turn sharply right and stay with this road as it meanders north and northwest along the right bank of Great Brook. About 3 miles from North Lovell, the road arches around to the left and becomes gravel surfaced. You pass several houses and a cemetery on the left. A short distance further on, you'll

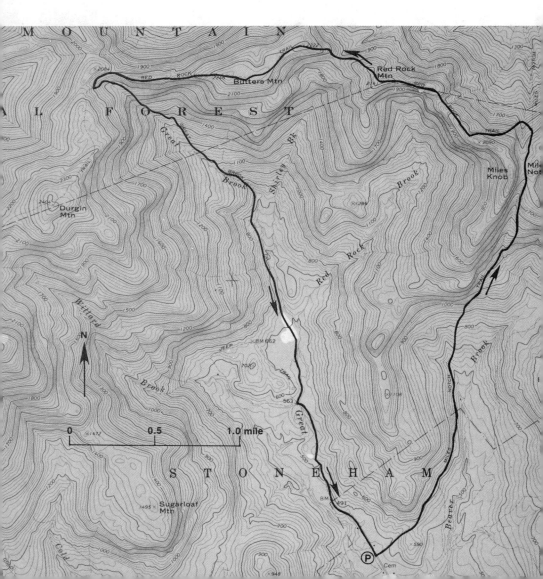

find the Miles Notch Trail sign on the right and, just beyond it, a grassy parking turnout on the left.

The Miles Notch Trail, first leg on your route, is an attractive, wooded path which connects, on the other side of the notch, with the Haystack Notch Trail in Bethel. From the Miles Notch Trail signpost, you cross a grassy clearing to the northeast, and shortly enter the woods. For the first ½ mile, you walk northeastward on nearly level ground through mixed growth. Beyond the ½-mile point, the trail follows the west bank of Beaver Brook, continuing northward. From here to the upper end of the notch you walk on easy grades in a cleft between the southern slopes of Elizabeth Mountain and the west flank of Isaiah Mountain. Approximately 3 miles from the road, you begin the steeper ascent to the head of the notch, which is reached in another ¾ mile.

From this high point (about 2000 feet), you turn west or left onto the Red Rock Trail, ascending just to the north of what was known as Miles Knob and onto the second summit of this same ridge, now called Elizabeth Mountain. The trail runs to the northwest here over ledge and scrub and descends slightly before climbing again to the summit of Red Rock Mountain. Views to the north open up here, and particularly striking is the sight of Caribou Mountain to the near northwest. Views south over the Red Rock and Shirley Brooks' watershed to Kezar Lake's Upper Bay are also pleasant.

As you hike beyond Red Rock, the trail proceeds northwest and west, dropping down several hundred feet before rising to the flat, ledgy summit of Butters Mountain. Haystack Notch lies immediately below to the northwest, under the steep defile of Haystack Mountain. You may also see East Royce Mountain, due west across Evans Notch Road 3½ miles away. Walk west along the ridge, arriving at a junction with the Great Brook Trail about 3⅓ miles from Miles Notch.

Durgin and Speckled Mountains are ahead to the southwest. Turn east or left on the Great Brook Trail. The descent here is rapid, as you lose about 1000 feet of elevation in 1¼ miles. Following the north bank of Great Brook, you cross Shirley Brook, which comes in from the left about 1½ miles below the ridge. Where Red Rock Brook joins Great Brook you cross the latter, pulling around more to the south and shortly emerging onto a gravel road. The trail now follows the road south and southeast back to your car, a distance of about 1½ miles.

Streaked Mountain

Distance (round trip): 1½ miles
Hiking time: 1 hour
Vertical rise: 750 feet
Map: USGS 15' Poland

Streaked Mountain takes its name from the strips of open ledges on its southwest flank. The short, interesting climb up the mountain leads to the fine views of the Presidentials and Evans Notch in the west, and to northern views toward Rumford and Weld. This mountain provides an ideal outing on those days when you don't have the time or inclination for something more ambitious, or you'd just like to sit on the ledges, basking in the sun.

The trail is quickly found by turning southeast onto a tarred road off ME 117, 5 miles southwest of Buckfield and 5 miles east of South Paris. A sign, "Streaked Mountain Road," marks this side road at its junction with ME 117. Follow this side road for just under 0.7 mile to where the trail runs east just beyond a culvert and under a power line. Park on the shoulder on the east side of the road. If you have trouble locating the trailhead, remember it is just northwest of the Becher farm, and is marked by a sign just in from the paved road. If you have passed the farm, you've gone too far down Streaked Mountain Road.

You first climb east-northeast along a grassy jeep road under the lines. This area is often overgrown with brush, but the trail can be easily followed if you stay under but slightly to the right of the lines. You shortly turn to the right, climbing steadily on the jeep path through low woods. A junction with three unused service roads is crossed in a moment, and the trail soon moves into the open again below the first stretch of ledge.

You climb steeply up the center of the ledge area, bearing gradually to the left near the top, where you pass through a band of trees. Good views to the west and northwest are behind you. A second ledgy bank appears beyond the trees. The route here also works to the left, passing through more balsam and arriving at the power lines just below the fire tower.

The tower on the summit rises above a series of antenna arrays and other unfortunate electrical clutter, and provides excellent views to the mountains in the west. Views range from Pleasant Mountain in Bridgton in the southwest to mountains in the Mount Blue area around Weld in the north.

Mount Zircon is north-northwest, and far off, to its left, lie the bold outlines of Old Speck and Baldpate. In the same

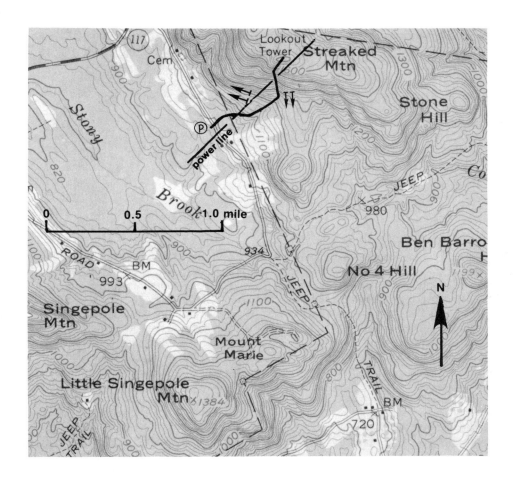

direction, Mount Abram rises in the foreground. Speckled and Caribou Mountains in Evans Notch are the two prominent peaks to the west.

It's all a splendid sight on a clear day and one you'll want to linger over awhile, before retracing your steps to the road. Lest you be reduced to dancing about and flapping your arms to keep warm, remember to pack a wool jacket along on even the balmiest days. Streaked may be a low mountain, but she's exposed to some mean winds that can make the summit a tough place to be if you're not warmly dressed, even in summer.

Burnt Meadow Mountain

Distance (round trip): 2½ miles
Hiking time: 2½ hours
Vertical rise: 1100 feet
Map: USGS 7½' Brownfield

Burnt Meadow Mountain offers hikers a fine walk, excellent views, and, most likely, plenty of solitude in west central Maine, near the New Hampshire state line. Burnt Meadow is one of those interesting but not-much-climbed massifs that, like great, half-risen loaves of bread, run north and south along the western fringes of the Pine Tree State in a kind of solitary splendor. With its three distinctive peaks, Burnt Meadow provides some marvelous sight lines over several dozen other hills that straddle this border country, including New Hampshire's Presidentials. Although this walk lies not many miles from the wearying commercial hubbub of what is called "Mount Washington Valley," it might as well be in another world, and therein rests part of its appeal.

Burnt Meadow was swept by a major fire in 1947, accounting for its young forestation, mainly deciduous woods, and considerable exposed granitic ledge. This young forest makes a pleasant change from the often-encountered dense coniferous forest in evidence on many Maine trails, and, if you hike in late autumn or early spring with the trees bare of leaves, the views are

even more spectacular on this walk. The route crosses no brooks or streams, so bring along plenty of water in your rucksack.

It takes a little back-road navigating to reach the trailhead on Burnt Meadow's east side. From the junction of ME 113 and ME 160 by a general store in Brownfield, drive west through the village on ME 160 for a little over a mile until the road makes a sharp left by the community church. Continue south on ME 160 past a cemetery and go by Burnt Meadow Pond. Two miles south of the church you will find a metal sign indicating Fire Road 145 on the right, where there is a shady turnout. Park here.

The trail, which is not visible from the road, leaves the turnout under a canopy of red and white pine and white birch, climbing the first of many ledgy outcrops dotted with haircap moss. Follow the blue blazes upward through a series of esses toward the southwest amid clumps of ground juniper and desiccated lichens. More open ledge is reached shortly with the first easterly views from the trail. Here and there are veins of quartzite and mica schist embedded in the host granite. A

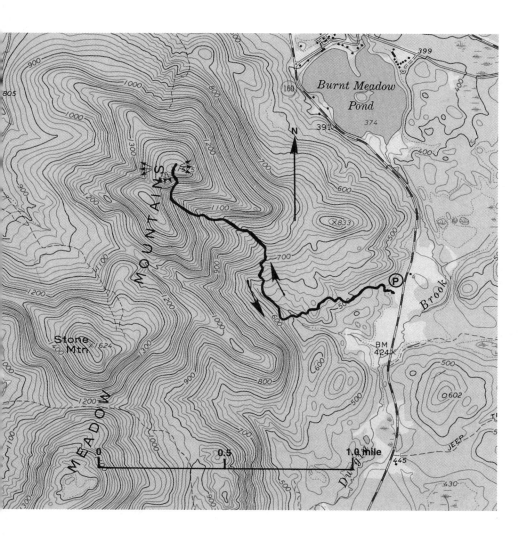

panorama of rolling green mountains gradually comes into view in a line from the southeast to the northeast.

The trail rises more gradually in groves of white oak, one of the deciduous species characteristic of this hike over once-burned ground. You pass a patch of common lousewort, and views to the north open up over your shoulder. Meandering more and more southwest, you walk onto a second series of open ledges with more expansive views. Staghorn sumac and limited red spruce are seen. In minutes, you reach a fine, open bluff with broad views to the valleys and mountains southward.

From this bluff, you follow the trail sharply around to the north and northwest as it ascends steadily through mixed hardwoods. Bearberry, goldenrod, and ground blueberries grow profusely along the path. Pass a pair of young hemlocks; the trail bears right and then left in a small clearing. Though it will probably be gone by the time you walk this path, I have seen here one of the largest hornets' nests I've ever come across in the woods. This one, probably made by yellow jackets or paper wasps and attached to a young cherry sapling, was the size of a football inflated to twice normal size. So elaborate and complex are these engineering marvels that it is hard to believe that they are used only one season and then abandoned, a new nest being constructed next season.

Beyond this bend a ledge takes you up and westward into a clearing bordered by mountain ash, hemlock, red spruce, white pine, and sumac; the ground is covered with weathered lichen. Excellent views to the south, perhaps forty miles into the distance on a clear day, open up as you proceed on near-level ground. Clumps of bearberries lie along the path now. The route rises again to the southwest and west.

Occasional glimpses of the second major hummock you'll climb on this hike appear to the northwest as the trail pulls rightward, crosses another level spot, passes a row of hemlocks, and descends past several large boulders deposited here as glacial erratics. The trail runs through a slump filled with spindly young ash, birch, and beech, and then rises very steadily west and northwest to more ledges with good views to the left or south.

The scramble over the middle hummock now begins as the route runs through ever-shorter vegetation and out onto open ledge bordered by thick dwarf oak. Ground blueberries grow profusely all around, separated by clumps of ground juniper. The main summit rises to the northwest. With the exception of a few wind-beaten pines,

vegetation here is low to the ground, shaped by the prevailing winds that come up from the valleys to the south. You can see far into the distance—from the southwest all the way around to the north. Four pairs of ravens (Corvus corax pincipalis) make soft quorking sounds as they ride the thermals near the summit.

The trail now runs northwest continuously, making the last steep rise to the summit. Scramble up a series of fractured granitic ledges. Black capped chickadees flit about a small stand of spruce. A final turn through the ledges brings you up onto the summit, where, by looking back toward the southeast, you can see the two hummocks you have traversed and, well out to the east, the road where you parked.

This is a broad, flat, open summit with mountainous views in all directions except northwest and north (views to the north are possible in spring, late fall, and winter, when the mainly deciduous cover is bare). In summer, sounds drift lazily up from Burnt Meadow Pond, which lies to the east below. A narrow grassy road meanders downward from the summit's north side, a remnant of the days when this mountain had a ski area on its northern slopes, now thankfully gone.

Though not a killer climb, Burnt Meadow offers mountain views from its 1600-foot summit that rival those of some of the more demanding hikes in this region. There are many pleasant spots around the summit to rest and picnic while enjoying the splendid outlooks, especially to the south where there is very little sign of human intrusion beyond a few scattered farms.

To the southeast, you can easily see the route you traversed on the ascent, and will now retrace. Dropping down into the trees again, you will reach the road in 45 minutes' steady walking.

Singlepole Ridge (Singepole Mountain)

Distance (round trip): 3 miles
Hiking time: 1½ hours
Vertical rise: 500 feet
Maps: USGS 7½' Oxford; USGS 15' Poland

Pink lady's slippers, an increasingly rare
flower in Maine

Old farmsteads, stone walls, geological oddities, and varied wildlife make an interesting but undemanding family hike up Singepole Mountain in Paris. In the heart of Oxford County, Singepole forms a low rise that can be managed by even youngsters, and thus offers good terrain for family outings and even cross-country skiing in season.

Singepole is approached via ME 117 from South Paris or Buckfield. Turn south off 117 just over 2 miles east of its junction with ME 119 in South Paris or 7.5 miles west of 117's junction with ME 140 in Buckfield. On this unmarked side road (numbered 5034, Brett Hill Road, which becomes Durrell Hill Road) go about 0.5 mile before forking left on a dirt road which you follow for another 0.5 mile to where a very rough jeep track departs to your left. Watch for an old cellar hole grown over with birches by the trailhead.

Your walk here is to the east along the jeep track, rising very slowly toward the abandoned quarry 1 mile distant. Birds and small animals abound in these woods. Coyote, deer, partridge, and rabbit may be seen along with a large variety of seasonal birds. You'll also come upon several meandering old stone walls constructed of local granite, pegmatites, and schists. Be careful in this section not to wander off the main track onto the various little side trails you'll pass.

Tramping through red and black spruce, hemlock, balsam, white and yellow birch, beech, oak, and pine, you top a rise in about ½ mile. Here, you'll pass through a circle of stones and over more eroded pegmatite. You shortly take a left fork in the track and move along to another clearing, grown over with plentiful blueberries and cranberries. Past some feldspar outcrops, you walk northeast to the old quarry site, now marked by signs of old blast bores and the quarry pool.

A rockhound will be right at home on this hill. White chunks of feldspar are easily collected, as are pegmatite (fused clusters of mica, quartz, and feldspar) and sometimes, tourmaline. Feldspar *(sodium plagioclase)* existed in commercial quantities on this mountain and was mined as recently as the 1970s, when the pocket proved to be too "rusty" to be commercially useful.

If you next walk right of the quarry and to the east, you'll head up to the higher of the mountain's two peaks. The route lies, again, over bare pegmatitic ledge and passes another small pool off to your left where further exploration for feldspar deposits was carried out. The walk now is to the east-southeast up the ridge to Singepole's 1420-foot summit. The trail actually dips slightly as it narrows in the woods just before you reach the partially wooded summit. There are good views over to Streaked Mountain (see Hike 4). To the southwest lies Singepole's lower but more open sister peak, where you'll head next by retracing your steps back toward the quarry. Just before you reach the quarry site, turn left and head south over the exposed ledge to the bald south summit.

Bold cliffs spill from this summit's southwest flank toward Hall Pond, the work of glaciation. Deposits of quartz, black tourmaline, and muscovite mica are embedded in the bare pegmatite. At the back of the ridge, the black rock that once covered the area—a common schist—can be found. Off to the southwest are the ski slopes of Pleasant Mountain. The White Mountains of New Hampshire lie to the west, with the Evans Notch region in the foreground. Over Hall Pond to the south you can see the long expanse of Thompson Lake. For a rather low elevation, Singepole delivers

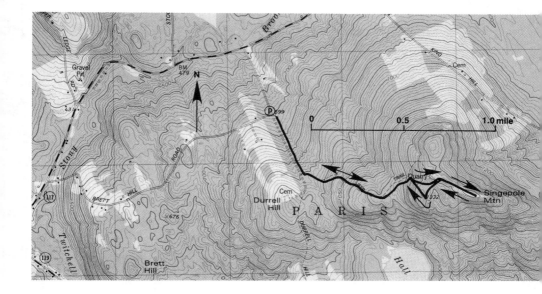

some very fine views over a broad expanse of western Maine country.

In returning to your car, retrace your steps off the south summit, turning to the left on a small trail downhill which shortly connects with the rough road you took to the quarry. Turn left again on the jeep road and walk west to your starting point.

Since most of this walk is gradual and in the open, Singepole Mountain can be enjoyed in the winter by anyone with moderate cross-country skiing ability. You may have to park out at the bend in the paved road, depending upon the extent of local snowplowing. In winter, with the trees bare throughout this hilly region, Singepole and its surrounding countryside are spare, cold, and beautiful.

7

Pleasant Mountain

Distance (round trip): 3½ miles
Hiking time: 3 hours
Vertical rise: 1500 feet
Map: USGS 7½' Pleasant Mountain

Pleasant Mountain is an impressive, rangy mountain that rises dramatically west of Moose Pond in Bridgton and Denmark.

On US 302, drive about 4 miles north and west from the center of Bridgton to the road which serves the ski area on the mountain's northeast slope. Take this road (the first left off US 302 after you pass Moose Pond) and watch for trail signs (an old pine tree with a red M painted on it at a gravel turnout) just over 3 miles south of US 302. Parking is difficult here for more than one or two cars. Make sure your car is fully off the road and not blocking the fire road.

The Ledges Trail, sometimes called the Moose Trail (hence the red M mark), begins its ascent from the east side of the mountain along the route of a gravel fire road. Red blazes mark the route for its entire length. You walk first northwest and west up the broad fire road, passing through patches of wild raspberries. Shortly the road narrows to a trail eroded by water. Climbing steadily west and southwest, you reach a fork in the road (which is again wider at this point). Bear

Northwest from Pleasant Mountain

left here, and—as you make an easy arc more toward the southwest—cross two small brooks in an area thickly grown up with young birch, beech, and cherry.

You then begin the steeper climb up to the ledges as you wind west up the ridge. At just under 1 mile, you climb over rock outcrops of Chatham granite which indicate the beginning of the ledges. Soon you move up out of the trees and merge onto the ledges proper.

There are fine views here to the southwest, south, and to the southeast over Moose Pond. You continue by climbing gradually around to the northwest, with the southwest hump of the mountain becoming visible through the young oaks along the trail.

You soon pass over a second open ledge area with good views to the west and southwest. Meandering first northeast and then northwest again, you climb more steeply over ground covered with low-bush blueberries, scramble over more ledge, and pass a third open ledge, which looks to the west. Turn northeast again, climb over a rock outcrop, and then turn north. In a few yards you'll reach the summit and fire tower on a grassy lawn that was once the site of the Pleasant Mountain House.

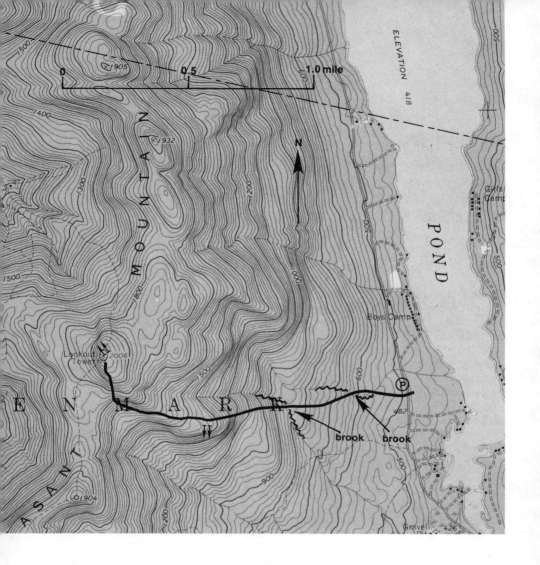

The views to the west and northwest from the "Green Pinnacle" are spectacular on a clear day. The Presidentials in New Hampshire stretch north to south on the distant horizon. Carter Dome is clearly visible over the west tongue of Pleasant. Tiny Kezar Pond and the narrow thread of Kezar Lake lie to the northwest, while Lovell Pond near Fryeburg can be seen to the southwest. The present fire warden in the tower welcomes visitors to his perch, but this, of course, is always subject to change. To descend, retrace your steps for a brisk hike of about 50 minutes.

Mount Cutler

Distance (round trip): 2½ miles
Hiking time: 2 hours
Vertical rise: 1000 feet
Map: USGS Cornish and Hiram 7½'

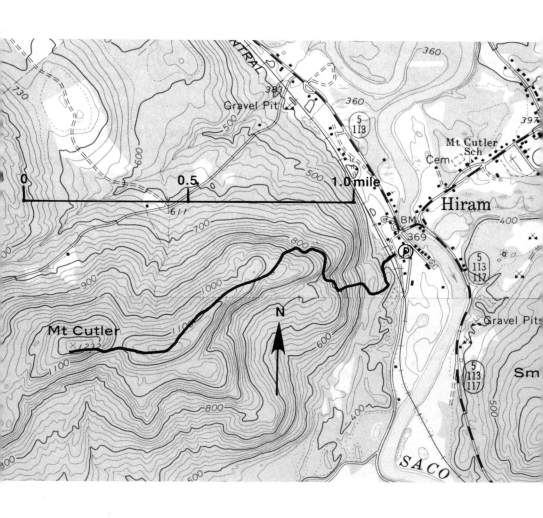

West of Sebago and looming over the banks of the Saco River, Mount Cutler in Hiram offers fine day hiking in a quiet corner of western Maine not far from the New Hampshire state line. This hogback provides some really excellent views for a relatively low mountain, and you take in the whole panorama of New Hampshire's White Mountains on this ridge walk. Hiram is a quiet, country crossroads, and it escapes the summer bustle of those towns eastward around Sebago. A visit to the village and the mountain offers an unhurried experience in a very attractive region of the Pine Tree State.

To reach the mountain, drive to the junction of ME 117 and ME 5 in Hiram where a modern bridge spans the Saco. On the west side of the bridge, go south on a local road to the village store, bearing immediately right on Mountain View Road. Just around the bend you'll find parking by some abandoned railroad tracks to the right of the road.

The trail lies to the left of and across the tracks from the parking area. You head immediately uphill to a grove of towering white pines. Shortly, bear *right* at a junction and proceed southwest on a tote road. Cresting the rise, this road ends at a small basin on the left, bordered by beeches. Big buttresses of rock and ledge are before you, and it's up these exposed granite arms the trail proceeds.

Passing the basin and the small, seasonal stream that drains it, head west and southwest as the trail quickly ascends. Zigzag over a series of ledges and follow the left bank of another seasonal brook upward into a ravine. In ⅛ mile, you cross this brook to the right by a large boulder in a tangle of blow-down. (Don't continue upward, to the left, on the apparent path of a little-used trail.) You now scramble up a steep dirt

track, turning gradually northward, passing directly under some ledgy overhangs. This route is erratically marked by red-orange paint blazes on trees. You must scout them carefully or you'll miss them and the turn just described.

The trail now slabs the lip of exposed rock as you walk northwest. Trail blazes are sometimes hard to spot, but the path is obvious as it hugs the edge of the hillside. Views over Hiram and the Saco begin to open up. You come soon to a more level spot in a grove of oaks. In winter, the trees are bare and good views northward toward the Presidential Range may be seen here.

You next turn sharply left and south-west under the oaks, and move quickly upward again in scattered young balsams and Norway spruce. Pass through several small clearings and the trail pulls around to the west, ascending more gradually over grassy ledge. In a few minutes you turn left onto open ledge with spectacular outlooks over the Saco River valley to the east, south, and southwest. This spot makes an excellent lunch site or rest stop before you move on. Douglas Hill lies eastward. The hills above Cornish form a ridge to the south. Heading generally southeastward, the meandering Saco bisects the pretty valley on its way toward the Atlantic.

To continue, follow the trail west and southwest as it winds through mixed growth along the spine of the hogback. Occasional open places provide an opportunity to gaze at the Presidential Range to the northwest. The massive, elongated summit in the foreground is Pleasant Mountain in Bridgton. The east summit of Cutler is reached about ¾ mile above the road, and, as the trail pulls around in an arc toward the southwest, you reach the main summit 1⅓ miles from where you parked. From

Summit View from Mount Cutler

the first height-of-land to Cutler's main peak, you cross open grassy ledges which are thinly wooded, offering more good views of the valley. Cutler isn't a high mountain, but this combination of light forestation and exposed ledge makes for striking, panoramic views that compete nicely with those of much higher peaks. The return to your car is made by retracing your route. Use care while descending.

The round trip to the main summit can be done in less than 2 hours, but it is wise to allow for a more leisurely pace. Unless you're used to such things, the initial steep scramble up to the ledges will slow you down, and it's prudent to allow extra time for this section, particularly if you hike Mount Cutler when snow and ice are present. Use extra caution if descending on ice.

South Coast
and
Camden Hills

Cameron Mountain

Distance (round trip): 4 miles
Hiking time: 2 hours
Vertical rise: 700 feet
Maps: USGS 7½' Lincolnville; Camden Hills Park Map

Cameron Mountain rests in the second rank of Camden Hills. Not among those that line US 1 and directly front the ocean, Cameron lies back in the woods behind the first range and orients itself more to the country to the west. Away from the human bustle of Camden harbor, Cameron makes a grand elevation for taking the measure of the Camden highlands and for blueberry picking in the bright, high breezes of a summer day. If you walk with young children, Cameron poses no problems, and the very gradual rise of the trail suits short legs very well.

Pick up a map of Camden Hills State Park at park headquarters just north of Camden center on US 1. Then drive 4 miles north on 1 to Lincolnville and turn left on ME 173, continuing 2.25 miles to a fork in the road. Bear left on Youngtown Road and immediately fork left again on unpaved Ski Lodge Road. Park just off the main road in the gravel turnout. Don't block the right-of-way. Walk southeast, south, and then southwest on the gravel way as it rises steadily. This road is often muddy in spring and rutted in late fall and winter. Hardwoods gradually give way to conifers as the trail hits higher ground.

At an elevation of nearly 1600 feet about 1¼ miles from the paved road, you arrive at a trail junction in a grove to the left. Here, a short trail to the summit of Bald Rock Mountain runs east. Across the road to your right, you must drop down into the scrub a short distance on a tote road to pick up the beginning of the Cameron Mountain Trail.

A Cameron Mountain sign across from the picnic area marks the trailhead, and from here you march north and rightward downhill through pleasant oak, maple, and birch cover. Follow the white blazes just 100 yards to a trail junction. Take the *second* trail to your left, the Cameron Mountain Trail, an old tote road which makes a beeline southwest for 1 mile to the mountain. You'll soon cross Black Brook as you move steadily southwest between the sunken remnants of old stone walls much in need of mending. If you walk this route in summer, take care with poison ivy, which grows plentifully in the road.

Abandoned apple orchards, cellar holes, and the relics of old farms lie here and there in field and brush. The trail stays right along the park boundary in this stretch, under the canopy of big black spruce, maple, cedar, and pine.

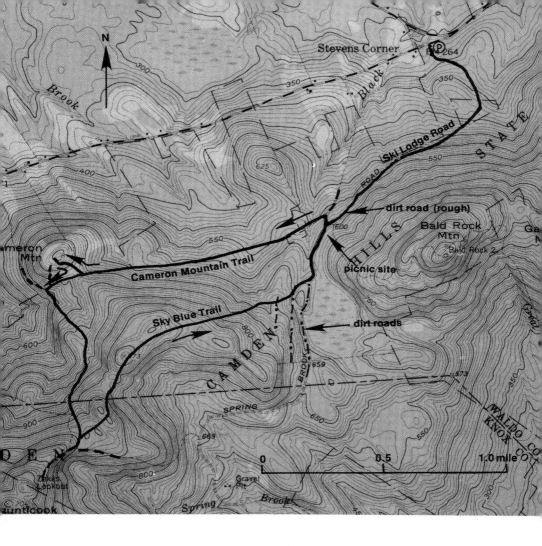

Cresting a rise, you will see the cleared summit off to your right. A farm pasture once occupied this space, but nature has reclaimed much of it, and the field now boasts only wildflowers and blueberries as its crops. Still, this open, breezy summit, just a few steps off to your right from the main trail, makes an excellent point to rest and perhaps fill a pail with berries. Meadowsweet, wild pink roses, daisies, yarrow, black-eyed Susans, and loosestrife grow wild.

Strawberries and lowbush blueberries dot the clearing.

If you look around, you'll see Levenseller Mountain in Searsmont to the northwest, and Gould Hill more around to the north over Coleman Pond. Bald Rock Mountain (see Hike 13) is close by to the east, and 1200-foot Mount Megunticook (Hike 12) rises due south. Hatchet Mountain and Moody Mountain make the north-south ridge that connects with Levenseller Mountain.

Penobscot Bay from the Camden Hills

When you've had enough of blueberry picking and want to move on, return the short distance through the pasture to the Cameron Mountain Trail, turning right at the sign reading "Sky Blue Trail—1 mile." You pass, on your right, another side trail to the summit and then bear *left* onto a small woods road. You are now on a connector route to the Sky Blue Trail, about 1 mile distant. You steadily gain ground, walking up Megunticook's north ridge in groves of mixed growth. Reentering spruce forest, you proceed up a series of natural stone steps.

When you reach the junction with the Sky Blue Trail, turn left and northeast. The trail moves over a series of low summits, pulling around to the north in about ¼ mile. After descending slightly, you rise again to an unnamed summit, just below 1000 feet in elevation. Descending gradually, you turn around to the southeast and then northeast again through black spruce.

This portion of the trail has been relocated in recent years. It rejoins the old path after reaching the flatlands along a marsh southwest of where you parked your car. Continue steadily northeast, being careful not to drift off onto several side roads in this area. Following white blazes, turn left on a dirt road, walk a few yards and bear left again onto Ski Lodge Road, walking the remaining 1¼ miles to your car at the turnout.

10

Mount Battie

Distance (round trip): 1 mile
Hiking time: 1 hour
Vertical rise: 600 feet
Map: USGS 7½' Camden

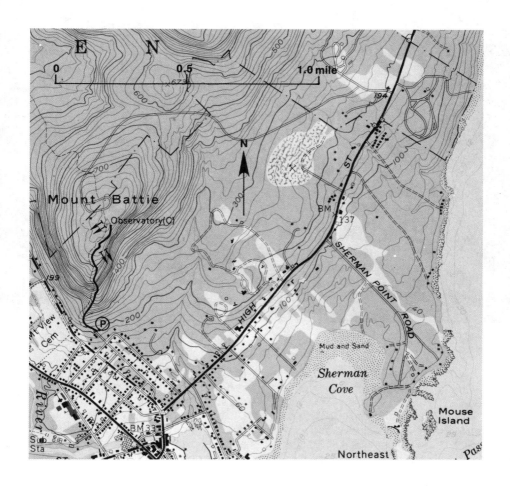

Camden Harbor from Mount Battie

Later in this book, I describe some of the exceptional climbing and hiking on Mount Desert Island in Maine. Mount Desert boasts the highest peaks along the North Atlantic seaboard and views to match. But because Maine is Maine, there happens to be a second excellent area of coastal hiking near what many consider the finest yachting harbor in the east. Camden, Maine, long recognized as the place "where the mountains come down to the sea," is the center of a ring of pleasant, low mountains that provide good hiking and views nearly comparable to those of Mount Desert.

A good first hike in the area, Mount Battie offers short, steep routes to exceptional views of the Camden Coastal scene. The Mount Battie South Trail rises from the northwest residential section of Camden, not far from the business district. The trail is reached by turning west onto ME 52 from its junction with US 1, just north of the town square. Take the first right, which is Megunticook Street, and follow it to a small parking space at the base of the mountain.

The trail starts behind a grand old Victorian house at the top of Megunticook Street. It's the house with the prominent widow's walk and the huge boulders in the front yard. A small parking space lies behind the house at the trailhead. Please be careful not to trespass on the grounds of the houses bordering this area and not to block the driveways.

The trail leads north from the parking area, climbing steeply up through mixed growth away from the houses. A series of S's are walked, with the trail rising steadily in the direction of the summit to the north. Deciduous growth gives way to red and white pine cover. Boulders, broken off from ledges above, are scattered about. The woods begin to thin out and views to the south open up. Looping around a ledgy outcrop, the trail winds upward, climbing out of the trees and onto a series of ledges which will characterize the rest of the walk. Pulling first to the left over exposed ledge, the trail winds westward briefly. A plateau is crossed, and the walk to the summit resumes with a further, quick scramble that will have you puffing. In minutes, the last rise is topped and you walk up through the low scrub to the bare summit. The whole walk up from the road has been just over ½ mile, but will seem longer due to the steep rise. The views here fully compensate your effort.

11

Maiden Cliff

Distance (around loop): 2¼ miles
Hiking time: 2 hours
Vertical rise: 700 feet
Maps: USGS 7½' Camden, USGS 7½' Lincolnville

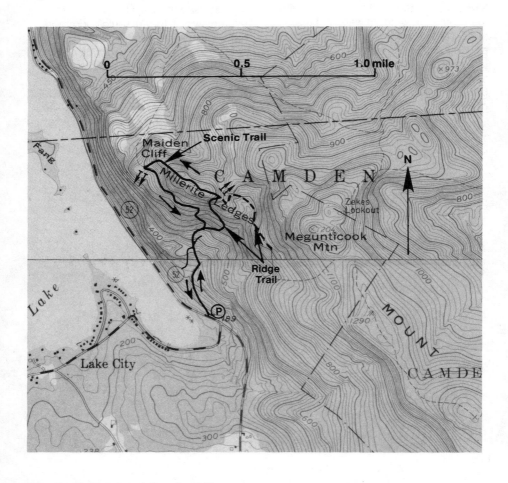

If sheer cliffs and picture-postcard panoramas appeal to you, the climb up Maiden Cliff, west of Camden, has something to offer both you and your camera. The cliff proves that some of the best views in the Camden hills are inland. Looming high over Megunticook Lake, Maiden Cliff—less romantically known as the Millerite Ledges—furnishes striking views to the south, west, north, and down on the extensive waters of the lake itself.

To reach the trailhead, take ME 52 west from Camden. Just before the road begins bordering the lake, 3 miles from US 1, a small, raised parking area, known as the Barrett Farm site, lies above the road on the right. Leave your car here and head north-northwest across the field into the woods. The trail follows an old logging road on a gradual rise through groves of beech and birch. The trail turns more northeasterly soon, and you walk above, and parallel to, a westward-running brook.

You cross the brook shortly on a weathered log bridge and climb to the left up the bed of another seasonal brook, going northward. Pulling into hemlock woods to the right of this second brook, the trail climbs around to the northeast, rising steadily in more coniferous forest. It's cool and shady in here in summer. You arrive, about ½ mile above the road, at a well-marked trail junction.

Go right at the junction and climb first easterly then north as the trail ascends quickly onto the higher ground of the ridge. You are headed toward what the marker below called a "scenic trail junction" with the Ridge Trail. As you ascend, there are open spots to the left of the trail with excellent views toward the southernmost Camden hills. Pulling steeply northeast again, you emerge upon some fine, open ledges with views eastward along Megunticook Ridge and over to Mount Battie. On a clear day, you'll see a good stretch of open ocean down toward Rockport and Rockland.

Continue a bit higher and you'll spot a junction marker where you bear sharply left and northwest on the Scenic Trail. Follow this path over more ledge and through the occasional slump as it meanders over the rock toward Maiden Cliff. The views here are spectacular to the southwest and northwest, and there are a number of excellent, open places to picnic where you can take the sun in mild weather. The white blazes lead along the edge of the Ledges and eventually curve downward to the west, where they lead to Maiden Cliff. The open cliffs are just beyond a trail junction, slightly off to the right through a grove.

A wooden cross above the plunging cliffs marks the point where 11-year-old Eleanora French fell to her death in May, 1964. Below you to the west lies Megunticook Lake. Bald and Ragged Mountains are to the southwest. Norton and Coleman Ponds lie to the northwest, beyond the lake. Far to the south, the ocean can be seen.

To return to the road, go back to the junction of the Scenic Trail and the Maiden Cliff Trail, which you passed minutes before. Go south on the Maiden Cliff Trail, walking first over fairly level ground, then ascending a series of steps. The predominantly deciduous forest of the upper slope gives way gradually to the conifers of the lower ground as you walk back to the trail junction first passed on your way in. The junction is reached in less than ½ mile, and you bear right and southwest, following the bed of the brook toward your car. Retrace your steps over the footbridge and along the woods road to the parking area.

12

Mount Megunticook

Distance (round trip): 5¼ miles
Hiking time: 4 hours
Vertical rise: 1190 feet
Maps: USGS 7½' Camden; USGS 7½' Lincolnville

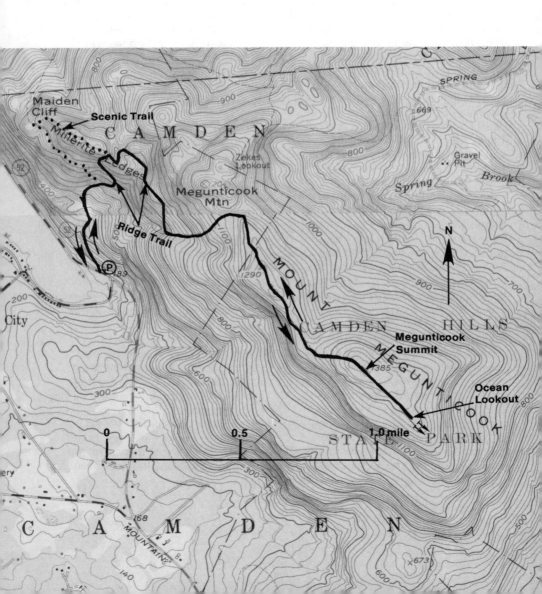

East shoulder of Mount Megunticook

A good part of the Camden area's best hiking lies within the Camden Hills State Park, which provides well-managed camping facilities at the very base of the mountain trails network. The park camping area is on US 1, about 2 miles north of Camden town center. The park office will provide you, upon request, with a good map of the local trails which will suggest other walks to complement those we have included here.

The broad ridge running from Maiden Cliff in the northwest to the state park campground in the southeast is Mount Megunticook. The mountain, highest in the Camden area and second highest on the northeast coast after Cadillac Mountain on Mount Desert Island, provides the best lookouts to the long expanse of Penobscot Bay. Ocean Lookout, about ⅓ mile east of the wooded, true summit, is our destination for this extended, 5-mile ridge walk.

Most hikers approach Megunticook from its busier east side. A quieter, longer, and highly scenic approach can be made from the west, and it's that hike we set out for here. To reach the trailhead, drive west on ME 52 from Camden center, parking at the Barrett Farm site about 3 miles west of US 1.

This route follows the same trail from the north end of the parking area as does Hike 11, Maiden Cliff. The rise is along an old woods road which follows a brook past a giant boulder and up into the woods. About ½ mile north and northeast above the road, you reach a trail junction in a hemlock grove. Keep right here and climb northeast and north as the trail rises quickly to the open ledges at another junction, where the Ridge Trail and the Scenic Trail meet. Pause here a moment to enjoy the fine views eastward. You can get a sense of the route ahead, for the long ridge of Megunticook stretches before you, and, off to the right a bit, you can see mount Battie with its distinctive stone tower.

From here on, the walk becomes more private. You drop eastward into mixed growth forest, curving gradually northeastward through low ground. The trail now begins to ascend a series of ribs as you start to gain altitude soon on the west flanks of Megunticook itself. The grades are not steep and your progress upward is steady. Deciduous hardwoods gradually give way to groves of hemlock, spruce, and balsam as you go higher. An hour and a half from the road (about 1⅓ miles), you arrive at a third trail junction in a shady hemlock stand. A trail runs north here toward Zeke's Lookout, Cameron Mountain, and Bald Rock Mountain.

Keep right in this grove, however, and go east and southeast on the Megunticook Ridge Trail. In mainly coniferous woods, the trail rises gradually past a series of lookouts with open views across to Ragged and Bald Mountains. Just over 2¼ miles from your starting point you reach Megunticook's wooded summit and a junction with the Slope Trail. Continue southeast and south now, walking the final ⅓ mile to Ocean Lookout.

Although the views along this walk are always fine, Ocean Lookout offers one of the best vantage points on the entire New England coast. Vinalhaven and North Haven are due east. Islesboro lies closer to shore in the northeast. Beyond Vinalhaven are the low shapes of Deer Isle and the whaleback known as Isle au Haut. Southward are superb outlooks over Rockland and Thomaston and on down the coast. On a sunny day, regardless of the season, Ocean Lookout is a natural place of great beauty to rest a while and enjoy the fruits of your uphill stroll.

The return is made by retracing your steps westward, remembering to keep left at the junction of Zeke's Trail and left again when you reach the junction with the Scenic Trail. This round trip can be walked in 4 hours moving right along. Five hours, with plenty of time for lounging on the open ledges, is a more leisurely estimate. And bring binoculars. Ravens are always busy in the air along the ridge, and hawks are commonly sighted.

.

13

Bald Rock Mountain

Distance (round trip): 3½ miles
Hiking time: 2½ hours
Vertical rise: 800 feet
Map: USGS 7½' Lincolnville; Camden Hills State Park Map

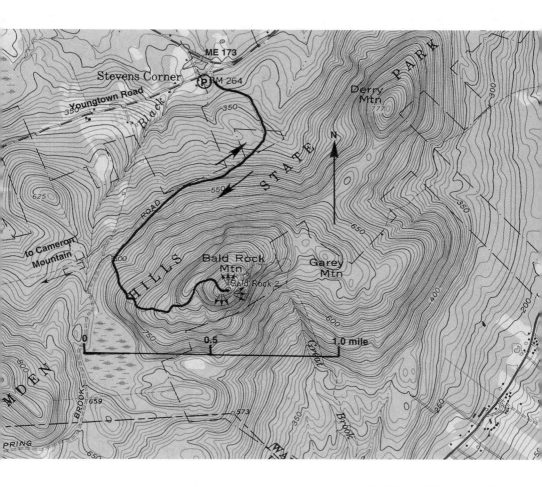

At the beginning of the hike up Bald Rock Mountain

This pretty, isolated mountain is at the northern end of Camden Hills State Park in the midst of the busy midcoast region. Bald Rock does not usually experience the heavy hiker use seen in those Camden hills which lie closer to the village. The woods around this 1100-foot mountain make for varied and pleasant walking, and there are good ocean views from the summit. Because the approach is gradual, this route can be hiked by families with children over 6 or 7 years of age without difficulty.

The path to Bald Rock no longer leaves US 1 on the east side of the mountain, but now departs from a point northwest in Lincolnville. The trail from the east side has been logged and posted in recent years. To reach the new trailhead, drive to the junction of US 1 and ME 173 in Lincolnville (4 miles north of Camden center), turning west on ME 173. Follow this road to a junction where you keep left. Just under a mile from this junction and 2¼ miles from US 1, bear left on Youngtown Road and immediately left again into a marked parking area that serves a network of trails. There is a trail information notice board and ample room to leave your car here.

You begin by walking through the gate onto a shaded tote road which runs southeast and southwest on easy grades. This is the old "Ski Lodge Road," which runs well into the forest to the site of a now-demolished building. In the past, the road has been open to season vehicle traffic (usually four-wheel-drive), but it is likely to be closed to motorized travel in hiking season. The mixed hardwoods found near the trailhead gradually give way to conifers as the trail rises to about 600 feet above sea level.

As the grades level out, you reach a junction approximately 1¼ miles from the parking area. Here, to the right, a trail leads to Cameron Mountain. To the left, you will head into the woods on a side trail to Bald Rock. Departing from a grove of tall conifers, the path now heads south and east in attractive mixed growth. A series of ridges and hummocks are crossed as the route climbs quickly, rising another 500 feet before

the trail pulls around to the northeast and reaches the summit.

The fine views from Bald Rock run north and south, taking in a grand sweep of the midcoast. The outlook northeast toward Isleboro and North Isleboro is particularly good. Looking due east on clear days, you may see Deer Isle further out. Hard to the southeast, you may be able to see North Haven and Vinalhaven, and, behind them, Isle au Haut, weather permitting. There are good views, too, down the coastal strip toward Camden. Many smaller islands are usually visible in the northern reaches of Penobscot Bay, and it is useful to have a chart of the bay along to help with identification. On fine summer days, there are more sailing craft than you thought existed, majestically plying these sheltered waters.

To regain the road, retrace your steps westward to the old Ski Lodge Road, and then turn right and north to the parking area.

Hikers may obtain a local Camden Hills State Park map that shows this hike and others in the area by stopping at the park gate on US 1, just north of Camden center. A full canteen also belongs in your pack, for there are no springs along this trail.

Ragged Mountain

Distance (round trip): 2¼ miles
Hiking time: 2½ hours
Vertical rise: 1000 feet
Map: USGS 7½' West Rockport

Ragged and Bald Mountains beyond Megunticook Lake

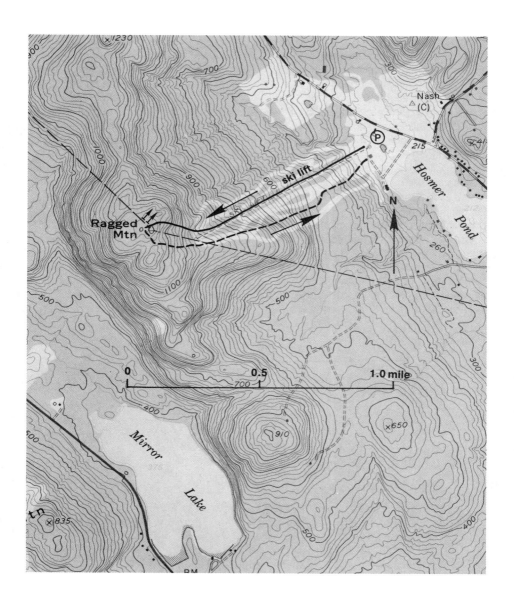

Ragged Mountain will give you a chance to look at the other Camden Hills from the southwest. Ragged also provides good views toward the Atlantic to the south, and toward inland Maine to the west. The mountain, home of the Camden Snow bowl, lies outside the state park area on private lands except for the summit, which belongs to the town of Camden. To reach the mountain, head west on Mechanic Street which begins in the Camden business district opposite Camden National Bank. The Ski area is just beyond Hosmer's Pond, about 3 miles from the town center. Turn left for the parking area by the ski lift.

There was, as of this writing, no regular trail from the mountain's base. The usual walk begins to the right of the ski hut as you look up the mountain. You walk up along the route of the ski lift to its upper limit, below the summit. This is a pleasant, sunny walk up grassy slopes that are ski trails in winter. At the end of the ski lift, turn right into the woods, watching for a trail that continues upward and swings to the southwest. Climbing through the woods, the trail shortly reaches the ridge connecting the summit (to your left) with the small, elongated dome to the north. Turn left on the ridge and climb over a ledgy area.

Shortly you'll reach the summit and its radio tower.

Looking south from the summit over Oyster River Pond, you can see the ocean. You look past Rockport to the Glen Cove area north of Rockland. To the northeast you may see Maiden Cliff, just on a line to the right of Bald Mountain, which rises in the foreground. From the cliffs, the long ridge of Megunticook runs southeast toward Camden. Mount Battie lies farther to the southeast just above Camden center.

The route down the mountain is a coin toss. You may head back the way you came, or proceed on the trail south beyond the summit, then turn sharply left down out of the woods and onto the ski slopes. Then follow the ski trail back to the ski hut at the base of the mountain.

Monhegan

INTRODUCTION

Of all the hiking routes open to the inveterate hiker in Maine, few are in so different and dramatic a setting as those on Monhegan Island. With its tiny sister island, Manana, Monhegan lies 10 miles southeast of Pemaquid Point and 12 miles south of Port Clyde in the open Atlantic. The island is reached by passenger boat daily (in summer, twice daily) from Port Clyde (the *Laura B*) and, in summer only, from Boothbay Harbor (the *Balmy Days*).

About 1 mile wide and 1¾ miles long, Monhegan is a community of artists and fishermen, numbering less than 150 in winter. The island population swells substantially in summer and, at the time of writing, three hotels and guesthouses accommodate visitors during the mid-May to Columbus Day season. Camping is not allowed.

The island has an interesting history. Its fishing banks were worked by European maritime powers as early as 1500. During the 1600s, Monhegan was the site of several short-lived attempts at settlement, with control of the island being contested by both the French and British. A pirates' base of operation in the early 1700s, Monhegan may have been visited by Viking ships around the year 1100.

Present-day Monhegan will be a disappointment to anyone looking for cute boutiques and nightlife. Blissful quiet (except for a foghorn) and a sense of slowing down, reducing one's pace, are to be expected on Monhegan. Besides its cottages and few hotels, the village boasts a sundries shop (island maps sold here), a single store, a chapel, and a little schoolhouse and library. Physically, the island is shaped like a giant granite whaleback. Its cliffs plunge abruptly to the sea, especially on the Atlantic side. A hill caps Monhegan's west-central section, atop which sits Monhegan Light. The built-up area of the island and its dock rest in a hollow below and to the west of the Light, opposite Manana. The village's one gravel road with its several spurs runs roughly north and south from the rise above the dock.

Although you can make a day trip to Monhegan in summer, you're strongly advised to stay at least overnight, and 3 days make an ideal visit. Be sure to make advance reservations. For information on boat

The Laura B., *Monhegan Island*

travel and accommodations, call the Maine Publicity Bureau in Hallowell: 207-289-2423.

A visit to Monhegan should take into account the very fragile ecology of the island and the reality that this island is often overcrowded with zealous day-trippers in high summer. This puts tremendous pressure on Monhegan's facilities and limited freshwater supply, to say nothing of spoiling the tranquil, remote peacefulness that is synonymous with Monhegan life. The advent of extra boat trips to the island in recent summers has increased the severity of this problem. Does this mean hiking Monhegan is out? No. I urge you to make your journey in May or September when the island is usually uncrowded and serene, and when accommodations are usually cheaper.

15

Monhegan South Loop

Distance (around loop): 2 miles
Hiking time: 1½ hours
Vertical rise: 50 feet
Map: USGS 7½' Monhegan

Nearly 20 trails link various parts of Monhegan, but there are two major "loop" walks on the island that include most of its spectacular scenery. The longer of these two loops makes a broad circuit of the southern end of the island and takes you by Lobster Cove, Christmas Cove, Burnt Head, and White Head.

To begin the south-island loop, start at the Monhegan Spa, above the dock. Walk south through the village, past the Monhegan House, and up the hill. Meandering by several houses, the gravel road continues southward, gradually running out into a grassy jeep track. The track ends above the rocky

Village shore, Monhegan Island

expanse of Lobster Cove, where there are good views west toward the distant mainland. At this point, a pathway, sometimes hard to find, continues eastward through the open, thick swale. To the south lies the small ledge known as the Washerwoman, and, ahead, a similar rock rib called Norton Ledge.

Following the edge of the land, you shortly turn northeast and north, passing Gull Rock. The trail climbs slightly, moving in and out of mixed spruce and balsam growth and over weathered ledge. The Underhill and Burnt Head Trails are passed on the left.

Continuing along the shoreline, the route next bends to the right around Gull Cove to 160-foot White Head, one of the two highest points on the island's seaward perimeter. The views are exceptional here, and there are a number of spots to stretch out and relax on the grass.

The White Head Trail, a grassy tote road, leaves the Head and runs nearly due west. Follow this road toward the village, and you'll soon pass a sports field on the left near the center of the island. Moments later, still walking west, you'll arrive at Monhegan Light. The lighthouse is a pretty edifice and, attached to it, you'll find an interesting small museum replete with exhibits on the island's natural and social history. Excellent views of Manana (now unin-habited) and the mainland are yours from the lighthouse lawn.

Continue westward on the now rather rocky road, which winds quickly down to a junction by the schoolhouse. Keep left here, and you'll come, in a few minutes, to your staring point by the Spa. Al-though this route can easily be walked in 1½ hours, so pleasant is it on a fair day that you may want to allow several hours and pack food and water along.

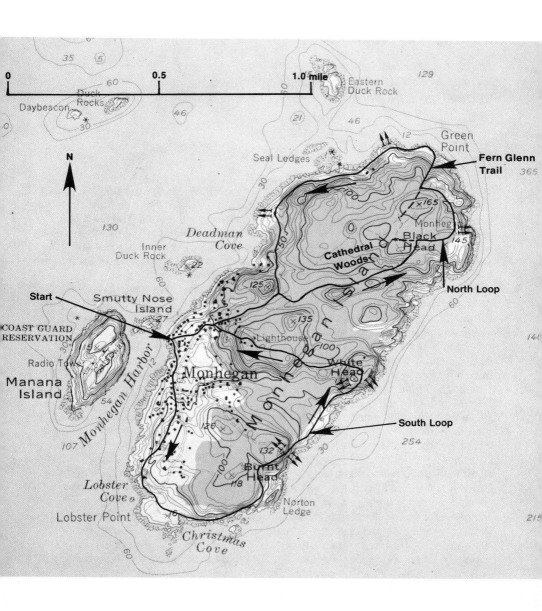

Monhegan North Loop

Distance (around loop): 1¾ miles
Hiking time: 1½ hours
Vertical rise: 100 feet
Map: USGS 7½' Monhegan

The loop around Monhegan's northern reaches provides an interesting hill-and-dale route through a landscape that is somewhat different from but just as attractive as the island's southern perimeter. This walk takes you through Monhegan's beautiful Cathedral Woods section and thence out onto the northern cliffs and rocks. Although this route can be walked in 1½ hours, the spectacular views and serene wooded areas will probably demand more of your time, and a leisurely walk of 2 to 3 hours makes a more reasonable schedule.

The Monhegan North Loop begins, as before, in front of the Spa, above the dock. From this point, head northeast on the gravel road past the schoolhouse. In about ¼ mile, the Cathedral Woods Trail (Number 11) is located on your right. Enter the woods here, proceeding eastward. The trail follows the north end of a kidney-shaped marsh to your right. Momentarily, you walk through Cathedral Woods, one of the most attractive spots on the island. The woods make a quiet sanctuary of tall red spruce, balsam, and pine. The trail is carpeted with fallen needles of these coniferous trees.

Your chances of coming across deer are excellent in this quiet, wooded part of the island. Many deer paths intersect the main trails of the island and are often mistaken for the trails. The deer paths are narrow and brush-choked, and they often end abruptly on a ledge somewhere, leaving you stranded. Stick to the marked pathways.

The trail next swings to the north as it nears Black Head and connects with the Black Head Trail (west) and the Cliff Trail (east). Turn right at this junction, following the Cliff Trail northward through the woods and along the headlands past Black Head and above Pulpit Rock. The route soon passes a junction with the Station Hill Trail, where you keep right, continuing above the water. Swinging westward, the more inland, you reach a "T," where you bear right on the Fern Glenn Trail (Number 17) and walk north to Green Point on Monhegan's north shore. This is the northernmost outcrop on the island. Turning west, it is only a short distance to Pebbly Beach. There are excellent views offshore to where Eastern Duck Island looms to the north, with Seal Ledges in the foreground.

Passing another trail on the left,

Fishing shack on Monhegan Island

proceed southwesterly along the shoreline, around Calf Cove. Nigh Duck and Smutty Nose Islands may be seen here lying farther to the southwest on a line with Manana. There are also good views of the mainland for the leisurely walker along these bluffs.

The trail moves away from Calf Cove and Deadman's Cove, turning now to the east and south. Your route connects with the Pebbly Beach Trail, where you keep right, turning south and shortly reaching the gravel road. Walk right on the road, pass the tiny schoolhouse again, and arrive in a few minutes at your starting point in the village.

Note: Climbing around the great sea cliffs of Monhegan's eastern headlands is a tempting pastime. The possibility of dangerous falls into the sea is always present, and given strong currents, isolation, and undertows, rescue would be unlikely. Hikers visiting the island are urged to stick to the regular, marked trails for their own safety.

Central Region
and
Oxford Hills

17

Mount Pisgah

Distance (round trip): 2½ miles
Hiking time: 2 hours
Vertical rise: 430 feet
Map: USGS 7½' Wayne

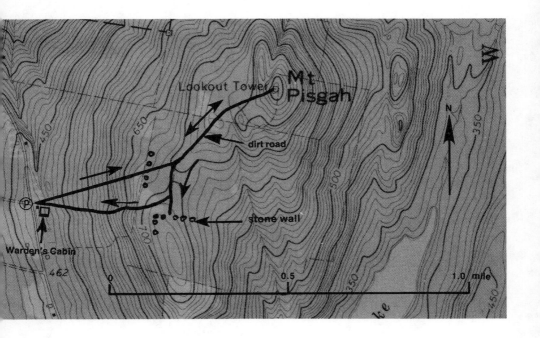

Mount Pisgah offers some easy hiking in south-central Maine in all seasons and is suitable for snowshoeing and cross-country skiing if the conditions are right. Located in Winthrop and Monmouth, Mount Pisgah remains one of a dying breed—a Maine mountain with a fire tower still manned by a warden. Years ago, dozens of Maine mountains supported warden-observers in towers from York County in the south to Aroostook County on the Canadian border. In his day, my father was a towerman, and patrolled the woods of

Family hiking on Mount Pisgah

the Rangeley Lakes region. My own childhood was filled with stories of northwoods life and tales of days spent in the towers of northwestern Maine. Needless to say, any mountain with a "live" tower on it is a good one in my book.

Drive to Mount Pisgah on US 202 west from Augusta to Winthrop, then turn north and west on ME 133 toward Wayne. Traveling just under 5 miles on 133, you bear left opposite Green True Road onto Fairbanks Road which becomes Mount Pisgah Road. Three miles up this road, you'll find the warden's cabin on the left. You can park either in front of the cabin or in a parking area across the road. A "Fire Tower" sign in the drive beside the cabin shows the way up a jeep track. Where a cable blocks the road, look for a spring that flows in the warm months, the only

source of drinking water for hikers on the mountain.

Beyond the cable, you walk the jeep track up a hill. You'll do most of your climbing on this walk in the first ¼ mile. Look behind you as you climb for good views above Androscoggin Lake toward the major ranges of the Maine–New Hampshire border; Mount Washington can be seen in clear weather. Your route is continuously to the east in this section.

Watch carefully as you ascend, for the trail departs from this gravel road and *enters the woods to the left* very suddenly not far up the rise. It runs under the power line in a northeasterly direction. This path continues to ascend over comfortable grades in largely deciduous growth. Passing through a stone wall, the path soon brings you out to a gravel road, where you bear left and follow this rutted right-of-way north-northeast for about ¼ mile, before the trail departs from the road leftward again back into the woods. The cover here is fragrant white pine. You pass through a brushy section and clamber over some ledges beneath the tower. In a few minutes more, you arrive on the summit plateau. Visitors are usually welcome in the tower, unless the warden is busy. Knock and announce yourself. Youngsters tend to find the opportunity to see how fire locations are plotted by triangulation fascinating, and forest service personnel are helpful in answering questions. I, for one, still find a visit to a fire tower intriguing, the only sounds being the winds in the stanchions and the squawk of the two-way radio.

Far north of Pisgah, you'll spy Bigelow and Sugarloaf in fair weather. Farther to the west, the Crockers, Mount Blue, Big and Little Jackson, Tumbledown, Bald, and Saddleback Wind trail off in the distance. From the south side of the tower, Pleasant Mountain in Bridgton is the most prominent rise. On good, clear days you'll be able to see Mount Desert Island and the hills around Camden to the east. Lakes Maranacook, Annabessacook, and Cobbosseecontee are below.

Heading back from the tower site, descend southwest over the ledge and into the woods on the trail by which you arrived. As before, you emerge shortly again on the gravel road. Take this road south, *passing* the point where the trail reenters the woods under the power lines. Continue south on the gravel road and you soon come to a junction. Keep left here as the road proceeds through mixed growth and small pastures grown up in ground juniper and blueberries. In minutes you arrive at a stone wall. There are fine views from this point over rolling pasture east, south, and southwest. The perspective is one of the prettiest in central Maine.

To descend, retrace your steps back along the gravel jeep road until you come to a junction that you passed earlier. Turn *left* here, and walk downhill to the warden's cabin and parking area where you started.

View west from Monument Hill

18

Monument Hill

Distance (round trip): 1½ miles
Hiking time: 1 hour
Vertical rise: 300 feet
Rating: Moderate
Map: USGS 7½' Pico Peak

Rising to the west over Androscoggin Lake in Leeds, Monument Hill is a low, drumlin-shaped mountain that affords an easy hike for individuals or families, yet offers some majestic views westward over wooded central Maine to the White Mountains of New Hampshire. Roughly 16 miles southwest and west of the state capitol, Monument Hill lies in the rolling farm country of south-central Maine in an area riddled with many lakes, ponds, and streams. This attractive hill is a highly visible landmark from nearby country roads and can be seen on the approach.

To reach the mountain, take US 202 to its midpoint between Lewiston and Augusta, a bit northeast of Greene. Turn north on ME 106 and drive just over 6 miles to Leeds. Passing a store on your right in Leeds Center, make an immediate left off 106 and up Church Hill Road. Follow Church Hill Road as it rises gradually westward and watch for the community medical center on your left. Just beyond the medical center, take a right on North Road. Continue to the trailhead about 1 mile north of this junction. A sign and several large boulders mark the trailhead. Roadside parking is available on the shoulder.

The route up Monument Hill has been modified recently. Some good trailwork now makes it possible to hike a pleasant loop over the mountain, returning to your starting point without retracing your steps. Begin by the boulders underneath the attractive sprawl of some great oaks bordered by a grove of beeches. A grassy woods road dotted with raspberry patches runs eastward and immediately passes another road that comes in from the right. Walking past this side road (follow arrow on tree), you continue east into a stand of hemlocks where the trail pulls southeast.

The path now becomes more stony and rises steadily in beech, hemlock, and silver birch. The walk continues around to the northeast, enters a cluster of pines, and soon levels off. The trail is marked by prominent gray blazes here. You next walk southeast through a corridor of low brush, past the remains of an apple orchard, and through further pretty stands of pine and birch. About ½ mile into the woods, pass a grassy road marked by a pile of stones on the right and continue southeast.

The road bends south through fragrant pines and balsams with thick ranges of ferns on both sides. Arching

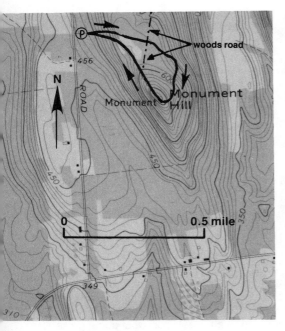

Mount Pisgah in Winthrop and Monmouth may be seen to the southeast. When more temperate weather prevails in July and August, patches of low-bush blueberries bloom around the summit, and you can easily spend a few warm summer hours here enjoying the splendid outlook to the west.

To continue the loop and return to North Road, follow the grassy tote road north and northwest off the summit. Mixed-growth woods, more blueberries, and ground juniper border the trail. Strips of granite ledge protrude through the grass underfoot. As the road descends, young black oaks are seen, and some limited views to the northwest occur. Gray blazes on the ledge outcrops mark the way as the trail climbs down quickly into some handsome deciduous cover. Enter a canopy of hardwoods and pass a road to the right as you continue downhill (left) in the direction of the arrow on a nearby tree.

Here and there the protesting chatter of red squirrels sounds in the trees. The road widens, dropping through strands of balsam, pine, and white birch. The familiar patter of black-capped chickadees and the plaintive peeping note of circling nuthatches is often heard. You soon pass the blasted skeleton of an old tree, and the trail bends left, then right, entering a corridor of superb old white pines where the air is pleasingly fragrant. Descending further through a low, grassy spot, you cross several log walks. In a couple of minutes you come to the junction with the main trail and turn left and west, arriving shortly at North Road.

Because this loop over Monument Hill is seldom very steep, it is an excellent snowshoe route or cross-country ski trip in winter. You should be prepared, however, for heady winds out of the northwest on the summit in the colder months.

right, left, and right again, the path runs up a slight grade bordered by oak, maple, and white birch. A series of exposed, gray granite ledges lies to the right. Shortly, you enter a clearing where, in any season but high summer, there are partial views eastward over Androscoggin Lake. The trail now pulls sharply right and runs up a short grade to the tall stone plinth, a Civil War monument.

Monument Hill's views are primarily to the west. Indeed, as noted earlier, they range from the nearby rolling hills of central Maine all the way into New Hampshire, where the Carter-Moriah Range and the Presidentials can be seen on the distant horizon. Maine's Mahoosuc Range lies to the west-northwest. More northerly is cone-shaped Mount Blue over Weld and, much further north, the four peaks of the great, east-west mass of Bigelow Mountain. In winter, with the trees bare,

19

Black Mountain

Distance (round trip): 3½ miles
Hiking time: 2½ hours
Vertical rise: 1250 feet
Map: USGS 7½' Worthley Pond

Summit of Black Mountain with Ragged Jack
in the background

Sumner is one of those nice little backwoods towns in the foothills of the western Maine Mountains where the flavor of a Maine that is fast disappearing still exists. And, on a dead-end road in farm country here, you will find Black Mountain, an inviting, low summit in the midst of the Oxford Hills. Black Mountain is sufficiently remote that you're likely to have the mountain to yourself on most any day of the week.

To find the trail, drive along ME 219 from either east or west, and watch for the junction of 219 and a side road which runs north to Peru a couple of miles east of West Sumner. This road is just under 4 miles west of the junction of ME 219 and ME 140. Turn north on this side road and drive 1.5 mile to a fork dominated by an old white schoolhouse with a flagpole. Bear left here and northwest on Black Mountain Road. This road forks in about 0.75 mile; you keep right at the fork and follow the road to the trailhead on your left just before the road ends at a farmhouse.

Your walk begins on a logging road which heads west and northwest through grown-up farmland laced with blackberry bushes. Stone walls border the trail. About ¼ mile into the woods, turn right by a lumbering operation site onto a narrower road and cross a small, usually dry brook. You curve right and more to the north here, ascending a slope grown up in beech, birch, maple, and oak. The trail has been deeply eroded right down to bedrock in places.

Ground cover is varied, including Clintonia lilies, blackberries, sarsaparilla, meadow rue, selfheal, cinquefoil, bluets, wild oat, and violets. At ¾ mile, the route levels off and pulls around to the right and east, soon crossing a brook bed, and then resumes its ascent. By any stretch of the imagination, you're in bear country and you may see tracks in soft ground.

At 1 mile from your starting point, fork left at a cairn and head north about 150 yards on a brushy, overgrown trail. Watch for the cairn very carefully, as it is easy to miss this turn, which leads you off into tall grass, through which no clear path is evident. Do not go right at the cairn where a newly constructed snowmobile trail leads off to the east and northeast to the summit of Allen Mountain. Turn right and northeast off this trail to another marked by a cairn. (If you follow the overgrown road left to a ravine, you've gone too far.) The route now rises quickly straight up the mountain via a gully to the northeast. Canada mayflower, bunchberries, and low-bush blueberries are found as you ascend. Most of the elevation gained on this hike occurs in this section as you zigzag back and forth across the mossy gully.

You wind shortly through sparse fir, spruce, and birch and reach a clearing dotted with sheep laurel, a flash of bright pink in midsummer. Follow the cairns over the ledges and through beautiful clumps of lady's slippers, which are in bloom from early to mid-June. About 1¾ miles from the trailhead, you arrive at the open ledges just below Black's wooded, 2100-foot summit.

The ledge is composed of the pegmatite so common in western Maine. Veins of quartz bisect the granite, and reindeer lichen shaded by fine spruce is in evidence. The views range from northeast to south here. Tumbledown Dick is seen over Mud Pond. To the east, you'll spot Ragged Jack and The Saddleback. Around in the south are Labrador Pond and the Nezinscot River valley.

Black Mountain may be worth several trips in various seasons. A hike just to see the lady's slippers (which are protected and should not be picked) is in order. The mountain's fine, panoramic

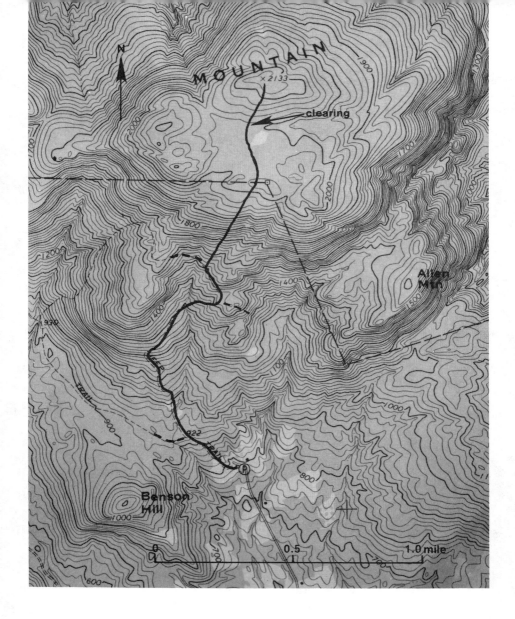

views are equally enjoyable in foliage season in late September and early October. Except for the brief sections where grades are prominent, the mountain can be snowshoed as well.

On returning to your car, be careful not to miss the turns on and off the old logging road at the midpoint of the walk. Since there are not springs on this trail, it is wise to carry some drinking water, whatever the season.

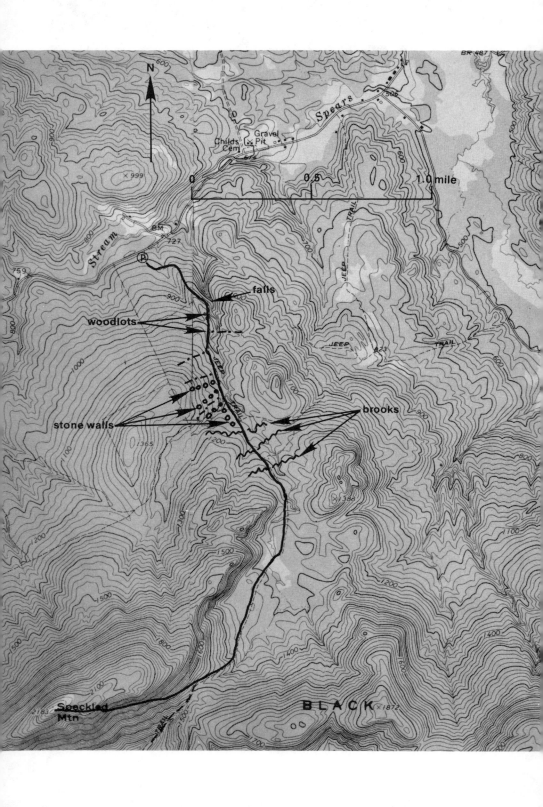

N

600

Spears

506

Childs
Cem
Gravel
Pit

× 999

0   0.5   1.0 mile

BM
727

759

Stream

falls

900

woodlots

JEEP

823

JEEP   TRAIL

brooks

900

stone walls

1365

1200

1300

1500

1388

1100

1200

1100

1500

1600

1400

1200

1600

1400

2100

Speckled
Mtn

2183

B L A C K   × 1872

BR 487

20

Speckled Mountain (West Peru)

Distance (round trip): 6 miles
Hiking time: 4 hours
Vertical rise: 1400 feet
Maps: USGS 7½' Mount Zircon; USGS 7½' Worthley Pond

A drive east on ME 108 from the paper-mill town of Rumford will bring you to the little village of West Peru and to one of the highest of the Oxford Hills, Speckled Mountain. Plunging, sheer cliffs and broad, open ledges characterize this excellent, remote walk high in the upper Androscoggin River country.

Arriving in West Peru, turn off ME 108 by a red cinderblock building which houses the local fire department. Continue on this side road southwest past a school and post office. The road rises gradually to the outskirts of town past the last houses until the area is heavily wooded. Approximately 4.75 miles from 108, the trailhead lies at the beginning of a brushy, grown-up logging road on the left side of the road. There is little room for parking here, and the hiker is best advised to park on the shoulder of the road, being careful not to block the right-of-way. The trailhead has no marker, and must be watched for carefully at the top of a rise.

The trail at first runs southeast and east through mixed hardwoods, which provide dense cover in summer. Striped maple, sometimes known as moosewood, lines the trail. The dark, striped trunks are easy to spot, as are

the oversized leaves in the familiar maple shape. About ½ mile into the woods, the slow rise of the trail ends, and you descend to the left along a waterfall on a tributary of Spears Stream. A short side trip to Spears Stream Gorge and falls is worth the extra effort.

Continuing now to the south, you pass through two woodyards about 1 mile from the paved road. An old road forks to the left across the brook, where you keep to the right, staying with the main logging road. The road follows the brook here for about ½ mile, coursing along through granite boulders. You soon pass the remains of a cabin on your right and also pass a fork in the road to the right.

In minutes, the road widens and views open up to the ridge on your left as you walk through clusters of waist-high cinnamon fern, capped with spear-shaped fertile fronds of cinnamon-colored spores. Two miles from the road, you arrive at a stone wall. The road continues straight ahead while another forks to the right. Here, you leave the road altogether, turning left and south off the road and into the woods, following the stone wall, which reaches three very small brooks in less then ¼ mile. From this point, the trail follows the red-blazed

Speckled Mountain behind Spears Stream

boundary line of Oxford Paper Company lands all the way to the summit.

Canada mayflower, trillium, and starflower carpet the forest floor as you begin the main ascent to the southwest and west. Hobblebush *(Viburnum alnifolium)* and young striped maple grow here, too. Hobblebush boasts a large, circular head of small, white blossoms like a bouquet in May. Come autumn, the berries become food for birds, including the wild turkey.

As you approach the summit, you move out of the mixed hardwoods common on this trail and into spruce growth. After bearing sharply to the right and west, the trail emerges onto the ledges. From here, you follow the edge of the sheer cliffs to the summit. Red blazes show the way through low blueberries and colorful bunchberries. The route ends just short of the west peak. It's an easy bushwhack to the top, through the best views are right here on the ledges.

The rangy summit of Bald Mountain (Hike 19) are visible. The views out over the precipice to the south and southeast are fine on a sunny day. On the descent, which follows the same route back to the road, keep your eye open for pheasant, partridge, deer, and other wildlife along the trail.

Evans Notch Region

21

Stone House–White Cairn Loop

Distance (round trip): 4¼ miles
Hiking time: 3 hours
Vertical rise: 1400 feet
Maps: USGS 7½' Speckled Mountain, Maine; USGS 7½' Wild
River, New Hampshire; Chatham Trails Association Area Map

The Stone House–White Cairn Loop over the south arm of Blueberry Mountain is arguably the prettiest walk in the Evans Notch region. Luckily, it's an easily accessible hike and, in the main, moderate enough in the demands it makes on the hiker to be open to all levels of ability. Nestled at the south end of Evans Notch, this approach to Blueberry Mountain lies between Deer Hill to the south, and the higher summits of Ames and Speckled Mountains to the north.

Like most of the walks described in this area, the Stone House–White Cairn Loop is reached from ME 113, the Evans Notch Road, which can be picked up either in Fryeburg to the south or to the north in Gilead at its junction with US 2. Watch for the Shell Pond Road on the east side of 113, 1.3 miles north of the AMC's Cold River Camp. Head on this dirt road by some mailboxes, pass through a cluster of cabins, and cross a wooden bridge over Bickford Brook. Immediately beyond the brook the road bears to the right and then bears left, heading east again. You stay with this

West from Blueberry Mountain summit

road for slightly more than 1 mile from the paved surface, and then park to the right just before a locked gate. Be sure to pull off the road so as not to block the gate.

The hike traverses the gravel road past the gate to the east as you pass through some pretty mixed growth and open field. In about ⅓ mile, you'll pass the White Cairn Trail on the left where it enters the road next to a couple of giant hardrock maples. Continue eastward, watching for the beginning of the Stone House Trail on the left just beyond a small white outbuilding. The turn is well marked. Please respect the privacy of the Stone House owners by staying off the grounds as requested.

The route now turns northeast over a winding logging road which sees occasional use. After several turns, the road passes Rattlesnake Brook Flume on the right. Take time to walk over to the stream, as the channel the water has chiseled through the granite is very much worth seeing. A footbridge also crosses the midpoint of the flume. Walking north on the trail again, a sign pointing to Rattlesnake Pool via a side trail is soon spotted on the right. Take this side trail approximately 150 yards

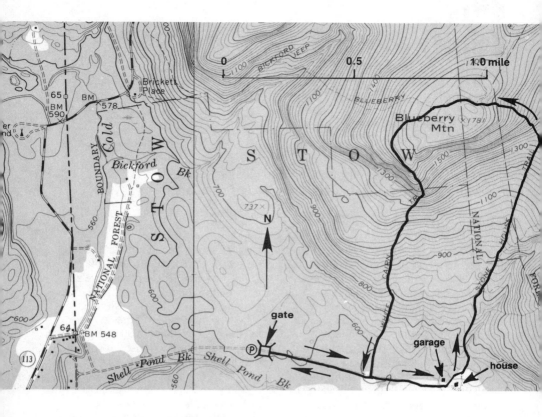

east to the pool and falls, which are even more attractive than the flume below. On a hot day, you may be reluctant to move on.

Resuming your walk, return to the main trail and walk northward on the tote road through young beech. The route rises gradually but steadily here, and you pass through a grove of balsam just under 1 mile from where you parked. Pulling slightly around to the northwest, you walk through more second-growth hardwood and bear left and west as the trail leaves the tote road and heads for the summit. The route now becomes quite steep, and the real climbing in this hike all takes place in this section.

Norway spruce form an arch over the closely grown trail as you move upward and to the west. Shortly, the trail climbs onto the open ledges of the summit. The Blueberry Ridge Trail comes in on the right and you follow it straight ahead across the broad summit. The highest point on the mountain is marked by a stone cairn where the Summit Loop Trail begins. This makes a good place to rest and enjoy the views to the north over Ames and Speckled Mountains (see Hike 22).

The Summit Loop Trail should be passed up in favor of a walk to the west ledges where the Blueberry Ridge Trail starts downhill. You will have to cover this ground anyway on your way to the White Cairn trailhead. Just continue to the west over the summit, dropping briefly into a wooded, boggy depression, and then out onto more granite. A sign indicates the White Cairn Trail on your left. Just ahead there are splendid views to the west and northwest from East and West Royce Mountains down to Mount Meader and the Baldfaces. On a clear fall day with the sun in the west, there are few nicer spots in Evans Notch than right here.

Backtracking a little uphill, bear right and south on the White Cairn Trail, which marches toward the lower end of the Notch over more red pine–studded ledges. You walk southwest and south descending quickly in the open. In ¼ mile you emerge on more attractive ledges with spectacular views over a sheer drop to the southwest, south, and southeast. Deer Hill lies due south with Harndon Hill and Styles Mountain more

around to the southeast and east. Shell Pond is the body of water to the southeast. The trail skirts the edge of the ledges, keeping this panorama in front of you, and then pulls to the east through a stand of white oak.

The trail drops down to the south abruptly, runs through a grove of red pine and then drops sharply again to the west. More on the level now, you meander to the south, crossing several logging roads which come in from various angles. Be careful not to get sidetracked here. The trail passes through a stand of tall, spindly balsams and then descends to a low, boggy point where it is crossed by another logging road. It is only another 100 yards before you emerge on the gravel road. Bear right for the brief walk back to the gate and your car.

Ames and Speckled Mountains

Distance (round loop): 8¼ miles
Hiking time: 5 hours
Vertical rise: 2150 feet
Maps: USGS 7½' Speckled Mountain, Maine; USGS 7½' Wild
   River, New Hampshire

At the southern end of Evans Notch stands a fine old brick country house, built in the mid-1800s. It is precisely the kind of place in which one would picture the hardiest of country types braving wild mountain winters. Certainly there was a time when such visions might have accurately reflected life here-abouts. Today, the building serves as headquarters for a Boy Scout council. But the countryside here in the Notch is as wild as ever. It is from the yard of the Brickett Place (as the old house is known) that you'll begin your ascent of Ames and Speckled Mountains.

You've room to park your car near the house just off Evans Notch Road (ME 113), about 11 miles north of Stow. The Bickford Brook Trail leaves the east side of the house yard, and rises quickly southeast and east. At ⅓ mile, your route connects with the Speckled Mountain fire road and turns generally northeast toward the summits. The fire road is a rough grass-and-gravel way, suitable only for the toughest of four-wheel-drive vehicles.

At the ½-mile mark, the trail levels off briefly, and the Blueberry Ridge Trail departs to the right. Continue up the Bickford Trail, and, at about ⅔ mile,

watch for a side path to the right which will take you out to views of the sand-and-gravel slides which extend down into the Bickford Brook ravine. Just above this side path the fire road crosses several feeder brooks, one or two of which are good sources of water even in dry season.

Another short side trail to the right just above here leads to good upstream views of Bickford Brook and its falls. You'll get a closer look at the Upper Falls at lookouts just to the right of the trail at about the 1¼-mile mark. Listen for the roar. (See Hike 30.)

After leveling off briefly, the trail climbs more steeply northeast, north, and northwest, making two S-curves between the Upper Falls and the 2½-mile point. You climb steadily through the curves, rising up through beech, a belt of evergreens, and then mixed beech and yellow birch. You'll travel briefly west along the ridge, and, turning northeasterly again, walk down through a depression where the sunlight is filtered out by densely grown balsams.

At 2¾ miles, good views of Mount Meader are to the west. The Spruce Hill Trail enters from your left as you approach the 3-mile mark. Although you

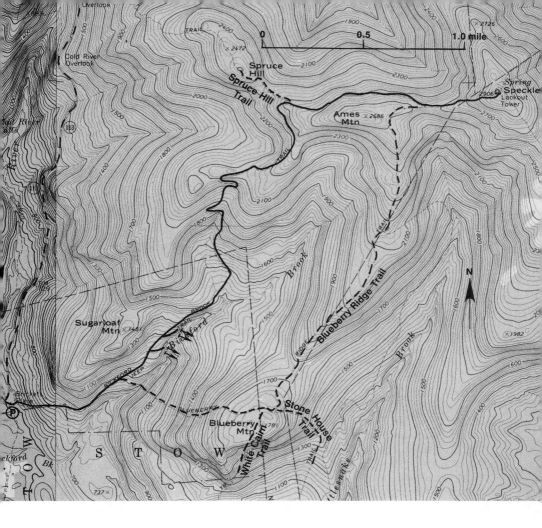

won't notice it, you'll pass the wooded summit of Ames Mountain in the next ¼ mile as the trail slabs eastward toward the summit of Speckled Mountain. You'll get partial views northward into Evans Notch along here.

At 3½ miles the Blueberry Ridge Trail appears on your right, just as you turn northeastward again for the final rise to the summit of Speckled Mountain. You climb fairly steeply here, past the last turnaround point for vehicles on the fire road, and move on to the rocky summit crowned by an unused fire tower.

The view from Speckled runs from northwest to southeast. The south side of the summit is wooded. The tower ladder has been arranged (as of this writing) so that it is impossible to climb up to where you could look out in all directions. What you can see from the ground is impressive, anyway.

East and West Royce Mountains are to the northwest in the foreground, and the Moriahs are just visible behind them and slightly northward. To the north, you can

Speckled Mountain in late winter

spot the Mahoosuc region; Goose Eye, in particular, stands out. As from Caribou Mountain (see Hike 24), Old Speck can be seen if conditions are right.

The horseshoe-shaped formation which is Butters, Red Rock, and Elizabeth Mountains lies to the east. Miles Notch is partly visible if you look to the easternmost end of the low range, where Elizabeth Mountain slopes southward. Looking southeast, you'll note two bodies of water: Virginia and Keewaydin Lakes.

If you return by the same route you climbed, the mountain provides an easy and quick descent. If you want to continue the "loop," go down the Blueberry Ridge Trail. You leave the Bickford Brook Trail about ½ mile below the summit at the marker. Your new route turns left and continues southwesterly. The trail rises and falls over a series of slumps for ½ mile, sometimes in the open and sometimes under the trees.

You pass shortly over open ledges where you should watch carefully for cairns, indicating the route of travel. There are good views in a southerly direction from the ledges. To your left, down in the ravine, is Rattlesnake Brook.

Now on Blueberry Ridge, you descend to a spring and then climb left to a junction with the Stone House Trail, approximately 2½ miles below the summit. The Blueberry Ridge Trail turns right, or westerly, at this point, passes a junction with the White Cairn Trail on the left, and descends westward to Bickford Brook. After descending for nearly a mile, you cross Bickford Brook and continue west. Climbing the westerly side of the ravine, you join Bickford Brook Trail again 9/10 mile from the Stone House Trail junction, and about ½ mile above the Brickett Place. Arriving shortly on the fire road again, you turn left (south) here for the short walk out to Evans Notch Road.

23

East Royce Mountain

Distance (round trip): 3 miles
Hiking time: 2½ hours
Vertical rise: 1700 feet
*Maps: USGS 7½' Speckled Mountain, Maine; USGS 7½' Wild
    River, New Hampshire*

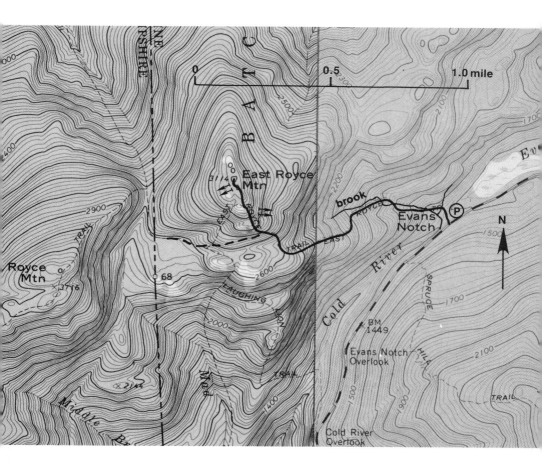

With a long enough arm, one could reach out from the summit of East Royce Mountain in Maine and touch New Hampshire air. No legerdemain involved. It's just that East Royce is probably Maine's westernmost elevation. The Maine–New Hampshire border falls between the two peaks of Royce Mountain, with the Maine—or eastern—peak rising imposingly by the center of majestic Evans Notch.

East Royce is not a mammoth mountain, given its immediate 4000- to 6000-foot neighbors, but from its 3100-foot summit, it offers superb views of the Carter-Moriah Range and of the Presidentials beyond. East Royce also provides an excellent outlook to the lower summits to the east in Maine. To the south are North and South Baldface, Eagle Crag, Mount Meader, and the Basin.

The East Royce Trail entrance is well posted on the Evans Notch Road (ME 113), about 3 miles north of the Brickett Place (see Hike 22) and Cold River Campground. There is room to leave your car just off the road in a grove at the trailhead on the west side of the road.

The East Royce Trail is barely under-way when it crosses the lower reaches of Evans Brook, a stream that begins up on the mountain and flows northerly into the Wild River and the Androscroggin at the head of the notch. After crossing the brook, you climb first to the right, and then left (west), ascending the clearly defined track of an old logging road.

In ⅛ mile a water-worn granite ledge marks the second brook crossing. Your path now swings southwest up along the left bank. Continue along the logging road, paralleling the brook and climbing steadily through stands of tall hard-woods and mixed birch. Shortly before you reach the ½-mile point, recross the brook again, turning sharply right (watch for a small arrow sign on trees). The trail moves northwesterly here over to the main tributary of Evans Brook. In sight of Evans Falls (high up on your right), the trail (you are still on the logging road) crosses a feeder brook, swings west again, and ascends an elevated rib of land between the two waterways.

Shortly after passing Evans Falls, the pathway crosses the feeder brook to the left, then continues right and westerly up through some fine silver birches as you near the 1-mile mark. Although the old logging road is easily picked out in this section, the brooks are dry in late summer. Brook crossings are less obvious. Watch carefully. The way is bordered on both sides here by hand-some clusters of both white and silver birch.

The trail and logging road climb up a steep rise to what must have been a loading area for timber up on the ridge. Birches give way to evergreens here. On the ridge, continue westward and climb through some stone outcrops and low evergreens. The grade here becomes quite steep for about ⅛ mile. The trail levels off briefly about 1¼ miles from the road, where it joins the link to the summit and forms a connector to the Royce and Burnt Mill Brook Trails.

Approximately ¼ mile below the summit, at the junction, a pronounced right turn to the north on a well-defined path begins the ascent of the open ledges that lie below the top. Watch for early southeasterly views framing Spruce Hill, Ames, and Speckled Mountains. On the final leg to the top, you follow painted blazes and cairns over the ledges to the northwest.

In the spring, the summit view to the

Southeast Face, East Royce Mountain

west reveals the Presidentials in fine alpine garb, white with snow. The summit of Mount Washington is visible over West Royce and Zeta Pass, between South Carter and Mount Hight. South (and left) of Mount Hight is the distinctive shape of Carter dome. Mount Madison lies west-northwest over North Carter. Adams, Jefferson, and Clay trail off to the west from Madison. Except for some low scrub which screens the view to the north and northeast, you can see in all directions here.

You pass from the south summit to the north crown by following the signs marking the path through the scrub. This short walk is worth the effort, as there are some splendid views to the north and east from the more northerly lookout.

In descending, follow the same route as you did coming up. Keep a cautious eye on the less prominent sections of the trail so you don't miss the turns and crossings.

New Hampshire from Maine—looking southwest from East Royce Mountain

24

Caribou Mountain

Distance (around loop): 7 miles
Hiking time: 5 hours
Vertical rise: 1900 feet
Map: USGS 7½' Speckled Mountain

Often, the rewards offered by a mountain are tied to the seasons; some mountains are best climbed at certain times of the year. Caribou Mountain, for instance, deserves your attention in late spring and early summer. Get yourself up into Evans Notch while the last of the snow is still melting, and you're in for something special. Two fine waterways border the trails that form the Caribou "loop." Before the warm weather sets in, these streams are running full tilt. They carry the snow-melt down the mountain alongside the trail. And, in mid-May, there are few places in Maine I'd rather be.

Morrison Brook and the Caribou Trail interweave nearly to the summit. Along the way, there are some truly scenic cataracts and falls. On the return loop, Mud Brook forms high on the south ridges of Caribou opposite Haystack Mountain and sticks close to Mud Brook Trail all the way out to the Notch Road. Together, the two brooks offer plenty of incentive to hike up Caribou and back, with the fine views from the top being just so much frosting on the cake.

The Caribou and Mud Brook Trails leave the east side of Evans Notch Road (ME 113) roughly 6.5 miles north of the

Brickett Place and 6.25 miles south of the ME 113–US 2 intersection in Gilead. This new USFS parking area is by the trailhead on the east side of the road. On the ascent, you leave the road and bear left, heading north and northwest parallel to the road. You shortly bear to the right crossing Morrison Brook and heading northeast and east toward Caribou Mountain. This is your first glimpse of a stream that you will rejoin shortly, and that you will stay with most of the way to the summit.

Now, proceeding east-southeast, you soon cross the brook again and climb along the east side of the stream. You'll cross several feeder brooks here as they flow in from your right. At slightly over 1 mile, you'll note rows of very tall, old silver and yellow birch. Birches of this size and vintage are uncommon.

Heading due east, you climb steadily now, slabbing along the increasingly steep rise to the right of the trail. Morrison Brook flows at the bottom of the ravine to your left. As you look down from above, the brook makes a pretty sight—particularly if you've come at the right time of the year.

From ¼ to 2 miles along the trail, you walk above a series of cataracts and

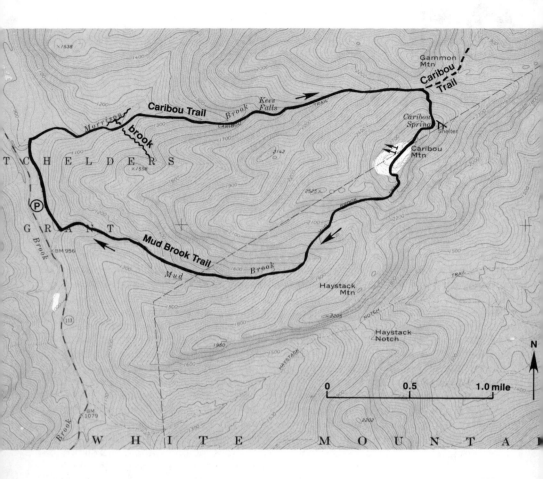

falls. Kees Falls is seen just past the 1½-mile point, with another cascade (high and to the right of the trail) not far beyond.

Crossing Morrison once more and continuing eastward, you ascend more rapidly now as the trail hugs the left side of the ravine. Good views to the south and southwest emerge, especially if you're climbing in early spring or late autumn. You cross the last feeder brooks which flow into Morrison at about 2½ miles from the road, and the trail levels off briefly above here. Climbing again,

you reach the col between Caribou and Gammon Mountains (watch for rows of stunted birch on either side of the trail). The Caribou Trail continues straight ahead to Bog Road and West Bethel. You turn right here on the col and ascend Mud Brook Trail to the summit, traveling south and then southwest. A US Forest Service shelter is located halfway between the col and Caribou summit and is a good place to camp if you're planning an overnighter.

Continuing south, you climb rapidly through birch and balsam to the first of

Morrison Brook, Caribou Trail

two open summits beyond the shelter. Proceed beyond the first clearing, which has views only to the northwest, and you'll arrive shortly at the true summit, which boasts a fine 360-degree view.

Speckled Mountain with its fire tower is the most prominent summit immediately to the south-southwest. Slightly to the left, you see the upper reaches of Kezar Lake and Horseshoe Pond. East Royce Mountain lies across Evans Notch to the southwest. Behind Royce, stretching south to north on the western horizon, lies the Carter-Moriah Range, topped by Mount Washington, still more distant. Peabody and Pickett Henry Mountains are to the immediate north. If you look between the two on a clear day, you'll see Old Speck far to the north.

To begin your descent via the second half of the Caribou loop, you follow the cairns south to an open, lower ledge, where the views to the south and west continue excellent, but become more sheltered. The trail meanders over the ledge, briefly turns sharply eastward, and then resumes its course toward the south and southwest through mixed scrub. Watch the cairns carefully as you descend the ledges; it is easy to miss the trail here.

You turn westerly, coming down amid tangled scrub and then through birch and balsam groves. At slightly less than 1 mile from the summit (2½ miles above the road), the trail crosses two feeder streams which will shortly become Mud Brook. The name is certainly a misnomer, for Mud Brook flows clear and clean from its origins to Evans Brook.

Beyond the streams, the trail proceeds west and northwest, slabbing the side of a ridge opposite Haystack Mountain. There are good views to the south here. The gradual descent continues, as you drop down among tall hardwoods and then walk southwesterly through stands of birch and balsam again. More feeder brooks are crossed (you are now about midway on the trail), after which a steep southerly drop leads you across the brook again. Skirting the west ridge of Caribou, the walkout travels in a northwesterly direction with mud Brook now on your left.

The final descent is gradual, and you pass through areas cut over for timber years ago. The route follows a logging road which intersects periodically with others, leaving open areas that have become deer pastures. Signs of deer are usually plentiful hereabouts, and you may be fortunate enough to spot deer as they come down to the brook at sunset.

You'll keep close to the brook as the trail nears Evans Notch Road. Mud Brook meanders to the south in a wide loop below thick firs and away from the trail momentarily. The trail pulls to the right and north in a recently relocated section, and makes its way to the parking area where you left your car on the right side of Evans Notch Road.

Recently, Caribou Mountain and surrounding woodlands have been granted a wilderness designation by the federal government. This classification will protect the "backcountry" flavor of these grounds and preserve them, unchanged, for hikers visiting in future years.

The Roost

Distance (round trip): 1 mile
Hiking time: 45 minutes
Vertical rise: 400 feet
Map: USGS 7½' Speckled Mountain

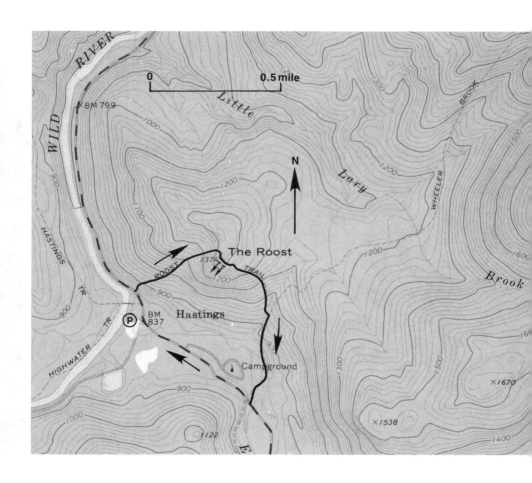

There is a kind of justice to mountain climbing: the excellence of the views you get at the top is often proportionate to the amount of effort expended in climbing up. Occasionally there are comfortable exceptions; the Roost is one of them.

The Roost is a small outcrop of ledge, a low summit, at the head of Evans Notch, offering very good views south, west, and north. And, it's all to be had for an easy climb. Indeed, there are many higher summits in Maine that provide less in the way of good outlooks.

The Roost Trail begins in the township of Hastings on ME 113 (Evans Notch Road), about 3 miles south of US 2. A spacious camping area lies just south on the Notch Road. The trailhead is located at the junction of the Wild River and Evans Brook, and a more appealing prospect would be hard to imagine. The brook stretches southeasterly toward the Roost and Caribou Mountain, while the Wild River curves upstream and westward toward its origins high in Perkins Notch at Ketchum Pond. Park off the road, south of the bridge.

Wild River, Evans Notch

Starting from ME 113 at the north end of Evans Brook Bridge, you ascend the Roost Trail directly up a steep, low ridge. Climbing northeasterly, you reach level ground briefly above the ridge, then turn easterly toward the Roost. Your route is through hardwood groves, with several giant, old white pines rising close to the trailside.

At ¼ mile, you cross a small brook entering from the left. You'll see a giant boulder here to the right of the trail. Climbing through tall white birch, you pass a low rock outcrop on the right, and then turn southward into a ledge depression surrounded by balsam and pine growth. This is the first of two ledges that form the Roost. A few yards southwest beyond this point, you'll emerge onto the true Roost, well above Evans Notch Road.

This 1200-foot-high ledge gives you an excellent view through the notch.

East and West Royce Mountains rise well to the southwest, across the notch. Howe Peak stands directly opposite your position. Behind Howe Peak, the Moriahs stand out. Look to the far left, southeast, for Caribou Mountain. To the northwest Baldcap and lower summits lead northeast to Mahoosuc Notch.

From here, there are two routes back to the road and your starting point. You may simply retrace your steps, and arrive back at the trailhead in about 20 minutes. Or, you may continue a loop that descends gradually from the south or far end of the clearing. This route runs southeast and south, gradually coming around to the southwest and emerging on ME 113 alongside a stream. Turn right on the road, passing the Hastings campground on your right, and you'll return in minutes to your starting place, about ½ mile north.

26

Wheeler Brook

Distance (full circle): 9 miles
Hiking time: 5 hours
Vertical rise: 1700 feet
Maps: USGS 7½' Gilead; USGS 7½' Speckled Mountain

This route at the north end of Evans Notch offers the hiker a variety of possibilities. With two cars, the trail can be done as an end-to-end walk from US 2 in Gilead to a parking area above Little Lary Brook in what used to be called Batchelders Grant. It is also possible to take the fine walk through the wooded hills that are a source of Wheeler Brook, descending to the Evans Notch Road, and then walking that road out to US 2 and back east to your starting point. It is this longer (9-mile) "circle" walk that is described here.

This route provides some climbing on easy grades, a chance to camp if you wish, proximity to several pretty streams, and a fine road walk along the banks of the Wild River. Evans Notch Road is not plowed in winter, and this route also can be used by showshoers and ski tourers who are well equipped and fully experienced at winter tripping. In spring, summer, and fall you may want to do sections of this varied and interesting trail as shorter hikes.

The trail begins on US 2, about 1.5 miles east of the Evans Notch Road intersection in Gilead. Parking is available at the trail head close to an old Colonial-style farmhouse. Watch

carefully for signs. Hikers should note that the trailhead area on US 2 may have changed. This spot has been in use intermittently as a military training area for several years, and some cutting of brush and building of parking areas may result in a minor relocation of the trail's entry point into the woods. Scout the area briefly when you arrive, or call the White Mountain National Forest headquarters in Gorham, New Hampshire for current status.

The trail begins on a woods road on the south side of US 2. Heading south, follow the road for about ½ mile. The road makes a sharp turn to the right, but you turn off on a path to the left and southeast. This route crosses Wheeler Brook and pulls southwest, gradually ascending the lower of Peabody Mountain's two summits. This is the highest point in the walk. The actual *second* summit is wooded, so there are no views at this point. (For clear views of this area see Caribou Mountain and the Roost, Hikes 24 and 25.)

Turning to the southwest, you slowly descend the lower reaches of Peabody Mountain, cross Little Lary Brook which flows into the wild river, and arrive on Little Lary Brook Road. This gravel road

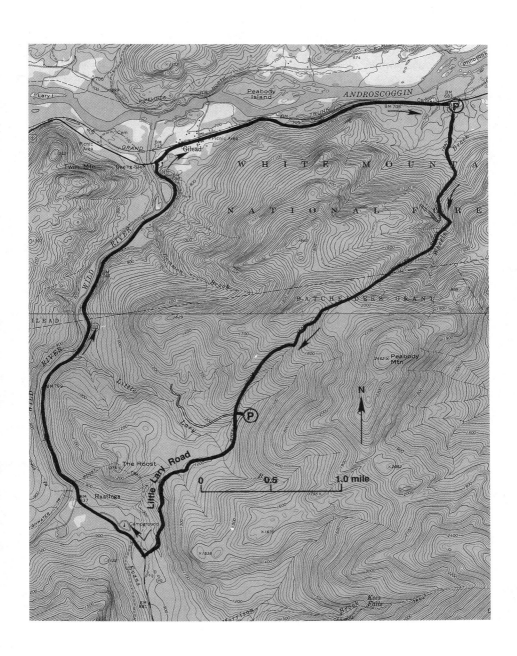

has been well graded and extended nearly to the west slope of Peabody Mountain to support lumbering and gravel mining. The trail follows the road from the mountain, through a gate at about 1½ miles from Evans Notch Road, and continues along the road to Hastings Campground. The road and trail join Evans Notch Road just south of the campground. At this point, you are about 5½ miles from your car via the tarred road. Campsites are available here in summer (check with the caretakers).

To return to Gilead, walk north on the Evans Notch Road. Very soon you come to the junction of Evans Brook and Wild River, opposite the trailhead of the Roost Trail. The river junction makes one of the prettiest sights in the notch. The river views continue as you walk north to Gilead, about 3½ miles from the camping area. At Gilead, a highway bridge to the left provides good views along the river, north and south. Turn right along US 2 at Gilead, and walk a final 2¼ miles to you car.

As I hinted before, this circle also makes a fine winter outing. A reliable ski-touring pack, with ski slots, is useful for carrying your cross-country skis and gear on the inbound trip over Peabody Mountain. You'll probably want snowshoes on until you reach Little Lary Brook Road. Swap your snowshoes for skis at this point, if you wish, for a good tour. Warm clothing, high-energy foods, an extra ski tip, and spare snowshoe bindings should be taken along for safety if you make the circle in winter.

Signs indicating the trailhead on this route seem to change often. A sign showing a hiker has usually been in place in the grassy field opposite the old house noted earlier. The actual trail sign was up in the woods. In recent seasons, a Wheeler Brook sign has been out near the road. As suggested earlier, scout the location for the current trail entry.

27

Albany Mountain

Distance (round trip): 4 miles
Hiking time: 3 hours
Vertical rise: 1100 feet
Map: USGS 7½' East Stoneham

Trailhead of Albany Mountain

Not many people think of Maine lands as being within the White Mountain National Forest (WMNF), but they are. In fact, of the nearly 730,000 acres currently within WMNF boundaries, almost 46,000 are in Maine. Although the highest mountains certainly lie within the New Hampshire acreage, I can only promise you, with necessary Maine stubbornness, that the prettiest part of the national forest is in Maine. If you've done some of the preceding climbs in the Evans Notch

Crocker Pond, Albany Mountain

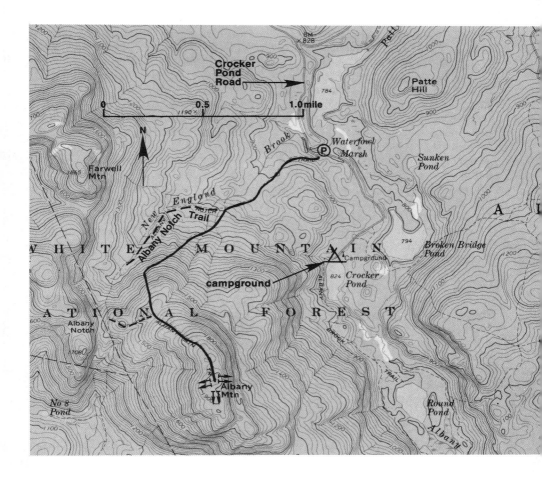

area, you know what I'm talking about. If not, the quiet beauty of the Crocker Pond–Albany Mountain area will convince you.

The Maine section of WMNF seldom gets the crowds that New Hamsphire does. This means you'll find it easier to camp on the Maine side of the border. And the camping, particularly at Crocker Pond, is good.

Located on the Albany-Stoneham line, Albany Mountain is a pleasant climb offering good views to the mountains in the Miles Notch area to the west. Camping in an attractive setting is available at Crocker Pond, just beyond the trailhead.

To reach the trail, turn south off US 2 at a store opposite the post office in West Bethel. At about 2.5 miles the main road bears right, while you continue straight ahead on a gravel road. The road shortly intersects another gravel way. *Continue straight on.* Approximately 4 miles from West Bethel, a well-marked entrance road to Crocker Pond leads to the right. Turn here, and in another 0.5 mile you'll arrive at the trailhead, which is prominently marked by US Forest Service signs. The Crocker Pond camping area is about 0.75 mile farther along this road. Park well off the road here on the grassy shoulder to the west of the road.

From the Crocker Pond Road, take the Albany Notch Trail west and southwest along a grass-grown logging road. The grade is slight to the ½-mile point, where the Albany Notch Trail continues straight ahead over a brook, and the Albany Mountain Trail begins turning left. You make the turn left (south), and ascend the north ridge of the mountain gradually, walking up through mixed evergreens and hardwoods. The area is thick with yellow pine. The Albany Mountain Trail continues southwest and then southeast as it approaches the summit.

About ½ mile north of the summit, a marked trail runs west to Albany Notch. The Albany Mountain Trail proceeds across periodic open ledges and through clumps of blueberry bushes.

Watch for any unmarked paths to the right here that lead to an outlook on the ledges to the west. You reach the summit about 2 miles from the road. The best views are from the ledges just crossed, with the hills to the west that form Albany and Miles Notches being most notable. Elizabeth, Red Rock, and Butters Mountains run west beyond Miles Notch, which is due west. Durgin and Speckled Mountains are the two higher summits to the west-southwest. Songo Pond in Albany is the body of water about 5 miles to the northeast.

Now, about those blueberries. If you've had the foresight to bring a pail up the mountain with you, the reward is at hand. A bushwhack around the summit will usually turn up enough berries for a good Maine blueberry pie or two. My problem has always been the picking. I hate it. Don't have the patience. But, if you do, and the season is right usually mid- to late July, you just may go away with a bucketful.

Retrace your steps for a leisurely walk to your car in about 1 hour.

Deer Hill

Distance (round trip): 4 miles
Hiking time: 2 hours
Vertical rise: 1250 feet
Maps: USGS 7½' Center Lovell, Maine; USGS 15' North
  Conway, New Hampshire; Chatham Trails Association Map
  of CTA Service Area

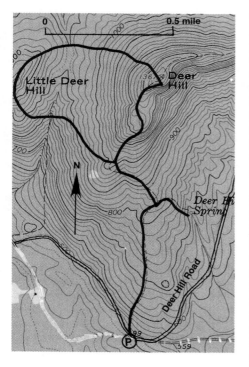

Big Deer and Little Deer are the two interesting summits of a rise known as Deer Hill in the midst of the intervale below Evans Notch. Two gem mines are

found on the mountain, as is a reliable limestone spring which furnishes very potable, cool water. Although a low mountain, Deer makes a fine lookout for examining the hills of Evans Notch area and the high peaks of the White Mountains to the west. Perhaps best of all, Deer Hill is set back in the woods off secluded ME 113, far from the traffic and noise of more developed tourist regions. When you want a quiet day in pretty countryside, try this route.

The loop around the two summits of Deer Hill is reached from either north or south on ME 113. If approaching from the north, turn south on 113 by the Wild River in Gilead. If coming from the south, drive north on 113 from the village center in Fryeburg. Turn east by a bridge over Chandler Brook approximately 13.5 miles south of Gilead or 1.75 miles north of the junction of 113 and the north end of the loop road to Chatham Center. The dirt road onto which you turn crosses Chandler Brook about 0.3 mile in from the pavement. This turn is 0.5 mile south of the AMC Cold River Campground. The AMC site makes a good point to inquire if you need directions or information on local trails during the summer months. You may also purchase a copy of the invaluable CTA local map here, too.

Drive east on the graded forest service road passing a small tarn. Passing several fields on your right, you will come, in a little less than 1 mile, to a prominent sign on your left on a banking that marks the trail to Deer Hill Spring. The spring, which is the source of Colton Brook, lies on your way to Big Deer summit. Leave the road here and head north into the woods, following the yellow-blazed trail up what once served as a mining road. Tall red pines and white birch border the route. You head uphill on easy grades for about ⅓ mile, leveling off shortly in groves of white pine, birch, and maple. Continue on this disused road, being careful not to turn into any of the several side trails, reaching a junction on a knoll about 1¼ miles from the spot where you parked.

Take a moment to make the short side trip to the spring by turning right here. Water in this unusually large spring is filtered through a vein of limestone, rendering it milky but very good to drink. Back at the junction, follow a trail northwest toward Big Deer. (Another trail here runs north along the tote road to one of the old mine sites and may be explored if you wish to add extra time and distance to the basic route described here.) Stay with the yellow blazes as you walk through old maples, beech, birch, and tall oaks. This more open woodland reveals wintergreen and spinulose woodfern scattered along the ground.

Shortly you ascend a ridge and emerge via bare ledges to an open knoll. The stony path here is comprised of pegmatitic granite, rich with quartz, mica, and feldspar deposits. Amethysts lie hidden and embedded in this once-molten rock. Here on the sheer south slope of Big Deer there are good views over to the White Mountains of New Hampshire, east to Harndon Hill, and over Little Deer to the immediate west.

Cairns and more yellow blazes direct you over ledge and through woods to another lookout over Big Deer's southeast flanks. Wild blueberries and clusters of trailing arbutus line the path. A beaver bog lies off to the east of the trail. A small mine to the north yields amethyst, feldspar garnet, muscovite, and pyrite. Across to the southeast are Harndon, Lord, and Pine Hills (see Hike 31). You can make out the long curve of Horseshoe Pond to the east of Lord Hill.

From this ledge, you walk up through bracken, fern, sheep laurel, and lady's slippers (protected) to the 1367-foot summit of Big Deer. Through the trees, the striking form of Baldface becomes visible across the valley. The trail now dips westward along the col to Little Deer. After some steep drops to the west and northwest, the route levels off in oak, beech, and hemlock growth and works uphill again to Little Deer after a steep stretch. Baldface, across ME 113, now can be seen clearly in all its rangy magnificence. You'll also see more of the familiar pegmatite here as this summit, like the others nearby, is part of the same metamorphic rock mass.

Two trails lead off Little Deer's summit. The one to the northwest goes to the AMC's Cold River Camp mentioned earlier. Take the *left* trail which runs south and enter the red pines and black spruce, descending toward the forest service road once again. Pass to the left of the Ledges Trail following the cairns down the open ledges. Soon you come to a trail junction. The route to the left runs east toward Big Deer, passing an abandoned mica and feldspar mine. Keep *left* here and walk southeast and east, descending gradually. This path carries you back, in about ½ mile, to the

Deer Hill, Evans Notch

trail junction you passed earlier above the spring. Continue to this junction, and descend southeastward toward the spring, the side trail to which you pass shortly. Bearing southwest and south you continue your descent, arriving soon at the gravel road and parking area.

Haystack Notch

Distance (round trip): 10½ miles
Hiking time: 6 hours
Vertical rise: 1600 feet
Maps: USGS 7½' Speckled Mountain; AMC Carter-Mahoosuc
  Map

The round trip through Haystack Notch amounts to a major woods walk of the kind increasingly hard to find anywhere. Though easily walked as a day hike, Haystack Notch lies in wild enough backcountry in the midst of high mountains to give you the feeling of a major expedition. And, if you plan it that way, the journey through Haystack can be extended to a 2-day hike, with an overnight at the Evans Notch end of the trail.

The route through the notch and over a col of Haystack Mountain is a point-to-point hike, running east-west and returning. The walk begins in Mason by the remains of an old farm settlement and runs west along the banks of the West Branch of the Pleasant River, descending gradually beyond Haystack Mountain to Evans Brook in Evans Notch, where it is possible to camp.

This hike makes an excellent walk for the amateur naturalist, too. Rocks, minerals, different bird species, wildlife, and mushrooms and various other fungi are plentiful, and you are very definitely in black bear and moss country while in

Haystack Notch Trail

the Haystack Notch area. You'll find this walk most comfortable in late summer and early autumn. The route crosses many streams, and the walking will be difficult and very roundabout in the wet weather of spring, when many of the brooks are sometimes very hard to cross.

The trailhead for an east-west transit of Haystack is found by leaving US 2 opposite the Post Office in West Bethel and driving south on Flat Road. Follow this road 6¼ miles, staying on the widest road into Mason. The road becomes gravel as it parallels the West Branch of the Pleasant River. Keep right at a well-marked fork in the road and you'll arrive at the forest service trail signs and parking area for both Haystack Notch and the Miles Notch Trail (see Hike 3). If you wish to hike this route in only one direction, you can spot a car at the other end of the trail on ME 113, 6 miles south of its junction with US 2 in Gilead.

From the trailhead, head west through a clearing and along the West Branch of the Pleasant River. In about ¼ mile, you pass old cellar holes of a farm settlement, and continue west and southwest on a tote road. Shortly, you cross the river several times, pulling gradually around to the southwest through pretty mixed growth. After walking 1¼ miles westward, you enter White Mountain National Forest lands. Rising very slightly, the route continues to the southwest, staying within the low point of the northern watershed of Butters and Red Rock Mountains to the south.

At 2¼ miles from your car, the trail crosses log culverts and begins to pull away from the West Branch. The grade now runs uphill more noticeably amid maple and beech, the ground dotted with doll's-eye or white baneberry. Several brooks, some dry, are crossed in this section. Given the variety of hardwoods, this march up toward the ridge of Haystack Mountain is particularly beautiful in foliage season.

Watch for old ax blazes on trees and small arrows as you ascend the shoulder of Haystack and emerge under the towering ledges of the mountain's south face. At the height of the notch, you are about 400 feet below the summit of Haystack, and at the highest point on this route.

You now descend to the west through aster, starflower, Indian cucumber, and wood-sorrel. The trail drops gradually west-southwest over the pegmatitic granite of the mountain and into scattered, very old giant maples, set back among granite boulders. Not quite 4 miles from your staring place, the trail crests a knoll, and a tributary of Evans

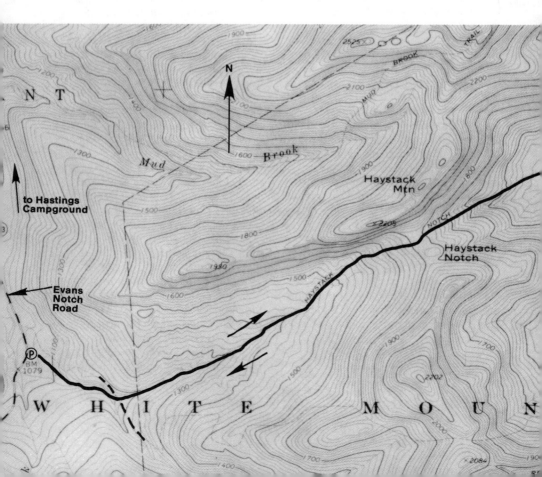

Brook comes into view. You cross this brook several times, finally bearing right and crossing the brook one final time. You continue west for another ¼ mile and emerge on ME 113 opposite Evans Brook.

A 2½-mile walk north on the Evans Notch Road will bring you to the campground in Hastings by the junction of Evans Brook and Wild River. It's a fine place to pitch the tent and rustle up some dinner. Technically, you can camp almost anywhere in the woods along the Evans Notch Road (ME 113), as it is all US Forest Service land. There are some restrictions, however, and fire permits may be required in summer. For information and permits, write or call: District Ranger, White Mountain National Forest, Gorham, NH 03581 (603-466-2713).

If you decide not to make this an overnighter and don't make the side trip north to Hastings and the campground (which is not included in the mileage estimate for this hike), you'll find plenty of good places to sit and have your lunch along the banks of Evans Brook before retracing your steps eastward to your car in Mason. Leave early enough on the return, which requires slightly more uphill work, to reach your car before dark.

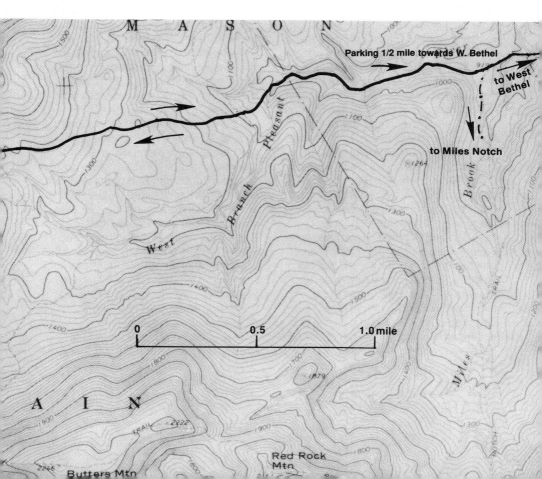

Bickford Brook Falls

Distance (round trip): 3 miles
Hiking time: 1½ hours
Vertical rise: 400 feet
Maps: USGS 7½' Speckled Mountain, Maine; USGS 7½' Wild
  River, New Hampshire

One of the most eye-pleasing character-istics of the Evans Notch region is the abundance of brooks, streams, and major rivers that flow through the area. The most striking ones are famous: Wild River, Evans Brook, Cold River, and Morrison Brook. Up in the woods, in the ravines between ridges and mountains, there flow some less-known but equally beautiful waterways. Bickford Brook has two distinctive falls which merit bringing your camera along.

Both falls are reached on the Bickford Brook Trail, which leaves the Brickett Place at the foot of Evans Notch on ME 113 (see Hike 22). From the east side of the yard on the Brickett Place, ascend the Bickford Brook Trail on moderately steep grades, running southeast and east. You'll join the Speckled Mountain fire road at ¼ mile. Turn right (east) on this road and continue the ascent.

Running together, the fire road and trail turn gradually northeast, climbing steadily. At ½ mile, you turn onto the Blueberry Ridge Trail, which is well marked. On the Blueberry Ridge Trail you drop quickly down to the east and southeast through tall stands of beech. Passing scattered evergreens, you bear

more to the left (northeast) and shortly arrive at the ledges over which the brook flows. Both sunny and shaded, these ledges furnish an excellent place to pause to eat your lunch by the stream.

Following the stream bank through the brush to the south brings you past a beautiful channel, gouged out by years of rushing water. Past the channel, the stream broadens out over open ledges where the waters plunge to the riverbed below. These falls are most striking in early spring.

Returning to the trail and your lunch spot, cross Bickford Brook where the trail comes down to the water. Do not head straight uphill once you are across, as that route climbs Blueberry Mountain. (This is a straightforward west-east hike of about 1½ hours round trip, and can be done as an extension of the Bickford Brook walk. Consult the map for Hike 21, Stone House–White Cairn Loop, which goes up the other side of Blueberry Mountain. The approach to Blueberry Mountain from the Bickford Brook side is very much worth doing if you have the time, energy, and inclination.)

Bear left once you are across the stream and head north and northeast on the remains of an open logging road. It rises gradually and then levels off as you follow the streambed on its right. A number of pretty pools lie along this section. A steep flank of Blueberry Mountain stays with the trail to your right.

Approximately 1 mile from your starting point at the Brickett Place, the trail runs *into* Bickford Brook, making its way across a chain of islands in the middle of the brook and continuing upstream (north). Watch for blazes on the trees, as it's rather easy to miss the turn off the stream bank. In another ¼ mile, Bickford Brook begins to run left. The trail now rejoins the right stream bank and heads up a short, steep rise. The route continues for a short distance on this rib, and in minutes Bickford Brook Falls pool appears on your left.

These falls, water streaming down from above over exposed granite ledges, make a beautiful sight, especially when the stream is at full spate in spring. If you wish you may follow the blazes down to the pool or continue

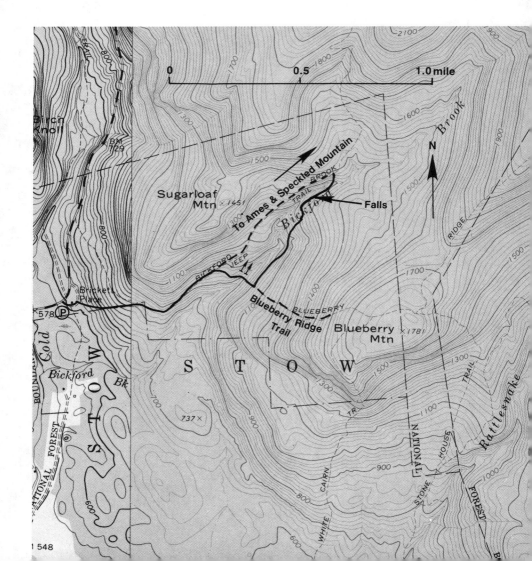

around the right bank above the pool where the trail eventually peters out beyond the boulders above the falls. This whole area around the pool and falls is worth exploring before retracing your steps to the road. If you've arrived on a hot summer day, the brook offers some very refreshing but very cold bathing. Bring your suit and test the waters before you plunge in.

Upper Bickford Brook Falls

Horseshoe Pond and Lord Hill, Conant Trail

31

Conant Trail

Distance (round trip): 5½ miles
Hiking time: 4 hours
Vertical rise: 1200 feet
Maps: USGS 7½' Center Lovell, Maine; USGS 15' North
 Conway, New Hampshire; Chatham Trails Association Map
 of CTA Service Area

The Conant Trail in Stow forms an elongated circuit over three 1200-foot-plus mountains in the border country of western Maine. Like its neighbors, Big and Little Deer (see Hike 28), the Conant Trail lies at the south end of Evans Notch on a Maine road that meanders in and out of New Hampshire. At the most easterly point of the Conant Trail there are some unique geological resources and fine views of beautiful Horseshoe Pond. This ramble through the unspoiled backcountry of the Cold River region makes a perfect day hike of moderate length.

To locate the Conant Trail, drive south from Gilead or north from Fryeburg on ME 113. Turn east on a gravel road at a bridge over Chandler Brook 13.5 miles south of Gilead, or 1.75 miles north of the junction of the Chatham Loop Road (north end of loop) and 113, 0.5 mile south of Cold River AMC camp.

Once on this forest service road, drive east, shortly crossing Chandler Brook and bearing slightly to the right as you continue to a point 1.5 miles from the paved surface. Here you turn right onto a narrow road marked with a Chatham Trails Association sign tacked to a hemlock tree. About 50 yards up this

side road, park your car at the trailhead.

With some water and perhaps lunch in your rucksack, follow the road as it works left and eastward to a clearing. Continue on to Colton Brook, passing a side road to your right. Cross Colton Brook, which has its origins to the north at Deer Hill Spring, and stay with the yellow blazes as you walk through hemlock and birch stands, your route bordered with some attractive old stone walls.

Passing a small cabin on your right about ¼ mile from where you parked, make a right turn onto a smaller road. The turn is indicated by a sign and blazes. This fork marks the beginning and end of a circuit, roughly 5 miles in length, over Pine, Lord, and Harndon Hills. You will come back to this spot on your return.

Wild sarsaparilla and bracken fern line Hemp Hill Road, along which you now walk to the south and southeast. Crossing a brook, you move through grown-up pasture land surrounded by mature hemlock and spruce. Tall oaks occasionally arch over the path. Stepping over another brook, you pass the cellar hole of the abandoned Johnson farm and immediately bear left off Hemp

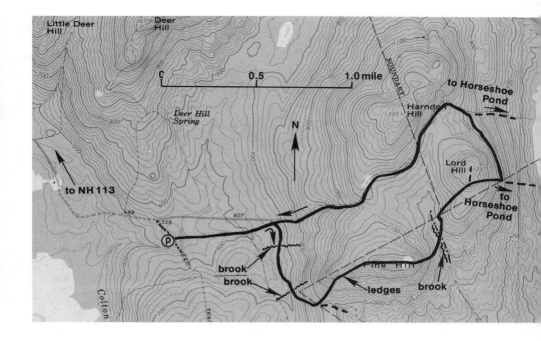

Hill Road. The path now runs northeast, climbing noticeably in white pine groves dotted with beech and oak. The Pine Hill ledges are reached soon, providing excellent views to the west over Cold River valley. You may want to stop here and rest a while, enjoying the view. Another good place to take a break is the open summit of Pine Hill, just a short walk further on through blueberry clearings above the ledges. Besides thick mats of desiccated lichen, the summit has isolated clumps of mountain sandwort, a tiny, white-petaled flower.

Here you continue downhill to the east over the ledgy eastern slopes of Pine Hill, with your next destination, Lord Hill, clearly visible in front of you. In the notch area between Pine, Lord, and Harndon

The view from Gilead

Hills, you will see the unmistakable work of the forester. More than 10 years ago, these lands were "regeneration cut." That is, undesirable brush and young growth were eliminated to make room for the desired white pine growth.

You momentarily reach the lowest point in this trail section by a small brook. A waterfall here channels the brook through mossy, granite boulders into a reflecting pool. Upstream, the trail crosses the brook, runs *across* a logging road, and heads up Lord Hill through scattered clearings speckled with low-bush blueberries, sweetfern, and bracken. You come upon the summit of Lord Hill in minutes: a small, open spot marked by cairns. A short walk toward the center of the hill (north) brings you to the abandoned Lord Hill Mine, but use a compass if you make this side trip, as brush has grown up and obscured the entrance to the mine.

This little "dig" has quite a history. The largest gem aquamarine and beryl crystals found in North America were uncovered here. This same potassium-feldspar ledge has been a chief source of topaz in Maine. The mine site can also be reached from a point further along this trail at the ledges overlooking Horseshoe Pond.

Resuming your walk, drop down to the eastern ledges of Lord Hill, where there are excellent views of Horseshoe Pond, a U-shaped body of water scooped out of the local terrain by glacial scouring perhaps 10–11,000 years ago. Departing the ledges, you walk southwest and left uphill for just a moment, then level off and bear sharply right heading downhill again, following cairns and a trail sign into the woods. In about ⅓ mile, you come to a junction where you have the option of taking a side trail to Horseshoe Pond and, beyond it, to the Styles gravesite. The Styles family were early settlers in this remote country, and were believed to have purchased 1000 acres of this hilly land for $1000. The side trip, if you make it, will add approximately 3 miles to the listed distance for this hike and an additional 1½ hours' walking time.

At the junction, take a left turn onto the trail for Harndon Hill. You circle the reforestation area, continuing along its border through beautiful stone walls and tall pines. Grown-up old pastures, now gone to ruin in sweetfern, blueberries, and brush, are crossed. The trail bears around to the west (left) and slabs the south side of Harndon Hill, rising to about the 1200-foot level in mixed-growth forest. Ascending gradually, you pass the old farm spring on your left. As this spring isn't reliable, you should always carry your own water on this hike. The old Harndon farmsite is here, too, half buried in woodfern and wild blackberries. A dense field of blueberries lies beyond the old cellar holes just before you reenter the woods, and offers excellent picking in early August. Harndon Hill itself has also been the source of fine gemstones, especially topaz.

The trail continues west amid blackberry brambles, and then widens and descends into shady hemlock woods dotted with violets. You are now on the old Harndon Hill Road which provides easy, brisk walking westward. A series of springs to the right soon becomes a brook which parallels the road. Passing through a clearcut, the road widens further, shortly passing a 200-year-old cemetery. Though badly overgrown, hand-cut headstones and gatestones can be seen. The thought of the families who settled here and made a stand against the mountain is a poignant one; their lives finished, the woods and brush have again taken over.

The Hemp Hill Road junction is reached shortly. You will bear right here and retrace the earliest part of this walk back to your car.

Note: As with Hike 28, a walk on the Conant Trail is easier if you have along a copy of the Chatham Trails Association local map, which was revised in 1988, and which covers the region in useful detail. The map can be purchased at the Appalachian Mountain Club (AMC) Cold River Camp buildings when they are open in summer, or from the AMC at 5 Joy Street, Boston, MA 02108, during the rest of the year. Some hiking stores also carry this map.

The Mahoosucs

32

Carlo–Goose Eye Loop

Distance (around loop): 7¼ miles
Hiking time: 6 hours
Vertical rise: 2200 feet
Maps: USGS 7½' Gilead, Maine; USGS 15' Old Speck
*   Mountain, Maine; USGS 7½' Shelburne, New Hampshire;*
*   USGS 15' Milan, New Hampshire*

The land area that lies north and east of the Androscoggin River along the Maine–New Hampshire state line is both wild and mountainous. The Maine side of this region remains the more isolated of the two. Thus, most of the good Maine climbing in this area is accessible only from lumber company roads leading in from New Hampshire. The Mahoosuc Range in Maine, from Mount Carlo north to Old Speck, lies mainly in lands owned by the James River Company paper empire. These borderlands are open to the public and, at present, permits or fees are not required by the owners.

Mount Carlo provides an excellent day's climb with fine views northeast toward Rangeley in Maine and also south toward the Moriahs and Presidentials in New Hampshire. This hike takes you up and beyond Carlo, along the Mahoosuc Trail (Appalachian Trail), to Goose Eye Mountain. It then heads southwest out to the road on the Goose Eye Trail. The loop makes for a trip of over 7 miles and some of the best views in the Mahoosucs.

Your route into the mountains begins

Goose Eye Mountain, Mahoosuc Range

in New Hampshire. From downtown Berlin, cross the Androscoggin River at the Berlin Mills Bridge (traffic lights) and proceed east several blocks, turning left on Hutchins Street. Follow this street through the pulp yards, across a railroad spur, then turn right on a gravel road known (but unmarked) as Success Pond Road. This 14-mile gravel road offers access to climbs throughout the Mahoosuc region. Indeed, except for the long, trailless walk-in from Ketchum via Goose Eye Brook or Bull Branch, Success Pond Road furnishes the only way into these mountains.

Watch for the Carlo Col Trail on your right, about 8.5 miles from the beginning of Success Pond Road. A grassy area to the left of the road will accommodate several cars. The trailhead lies opposite this point. A white sign marks the trail at present.

Both the Carlo Col Trail and the Goose Eye Trail run together for a short distance, heading eastward. At the Brown Company woodlands sign, you turn sharply right on the Carlo Col Trail and cross a brook. After you scramble up the opposite bank, bear left on the trail, which now follows an old logging road running south-southeast.

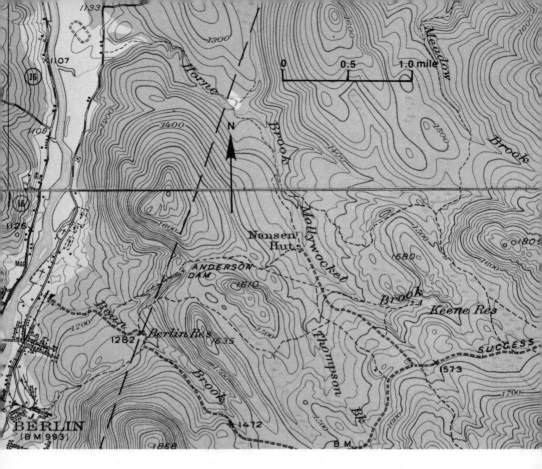

At ⅔ mile, you walk more toward the south as the trail pulls away from the south branch of Stearns Brook, which it has followed to this point. A feeder brook joins the trail a short distance above this turn. You enter a clearing where logging roads intersect at ¾ mile. The col between Mount Carlo and Mount Success is visible high up ahead. Keeping to the left, you cross the brook here and climb easily through young cherry growth. In among the young trees in this field-returning-to-woods, I have seen many clear moose tracks. Though the field is removed from the swamp browse that moose love, this seems to

be a well-used area. Keep your eyes open.

You now begin to climb more steeply, slabbing up a ridge and moving past the junction (left) of another logging road. From here, your route makes a beeline straight for the col.

The logging road diminishes to only a wide path at 1¾ miles, where you cross a small brook. There are several old pines that have grown atop boulders in this section of the trail.

You cross another small brook at the 2-mile mark, and the steeper ascent of the col itself begins. The trail winds up through stands of white birch and fir

here. A third brook is crossed as you swing more toward the summit of Carlo. Good views of the northwest ridge of Mount Success emerge behind you at this point.

The Carlo Col Shelter stands on your left up on a bluff as you reach a spot ¼ mile below the highest point on the col. Continuing, you soon reach the Mahoosuc Trail in a sharp rock cut at 2⅔ miles. The route to Carlo and Goose Eye turns left. Bearing left, ascend northeasterly on a steep grade for ½ mile through close-grown red and black spruce to the Carlo summit.

Scattered low scrub grows around the summit of Carlo. You'll need to move around some to gain outlooks in all directions. To the north is the horn of Goose Eye Mountain. The Mahoosuc Trail proceeds northeast across the sedge.

You may want to make an overnighter of this trip, descending again to Carlo Col Shelter for the night. Sleeping space in the shelter is limited, but there are spaces for tents, too. Whether you camp overnight or proceed to Goose Eye the same day, head northeast on the Mahoosuc Trail once underway. The trail winds beyond Carlo's summit and enters low evergreens again. You soon pass over the wooded north summit of Carlo and then descend sharply to a col. The trail traverses a series of ledgy areas and low cliffs as it climbs rapidly up the south ridge of Goose Eye. The going here is quite steep, sometimes requiring handholds. Reaching the bare south shoulder of the Eye, you turn left on the Goose Eye Trail to the west summit of the mountain, which you'll reach in a few yards. Total distance from the top of Carlo to the west peak of Goose Eye adds up to about 1½ miles.

To regain the road, continue the loop by heading down northwestward along the Goose Eye Trail. Use caution on the descent of this steep, ledgy ridge just below the summit. Continuing toward the northwest, you enter the woods. The trail soon bears more to the west as it drops down toward the road on a comfortable grade. Slightly over 1 mile below the summit, the trail makes a sharp turn to the left (southwest) through country well populated with moose. The spruce and balsam that characterize the upper slopes now give way to hardwoods.

Gradually turning more toward the northwest again, you join the roadbed of an old logging railroad about 1 mile above the road. Here you turn again sharply toward the southwest and, following the old railroad bed, shortly reach Success Pond Road and your car.

Note: If it is storming with high winds, don't attempt to climb the exposed area below the summit of Goose Eye. Rather, head down below the timberline, retracing your route on the Carlo Col Trail.

Mahoosuc Notch and Speck Pond Loop

Distance (around loop): 11 miles
Hiking time: 9 hours
Vertical rise: 2300 feet
Maps: USGS 15' Old Speck Mountain, Maine; USGS 7½'
  Gilead, Maine; USGS 15' Milan, New Hampshire; USGS 7½'
  Shelburne, New Hampshire

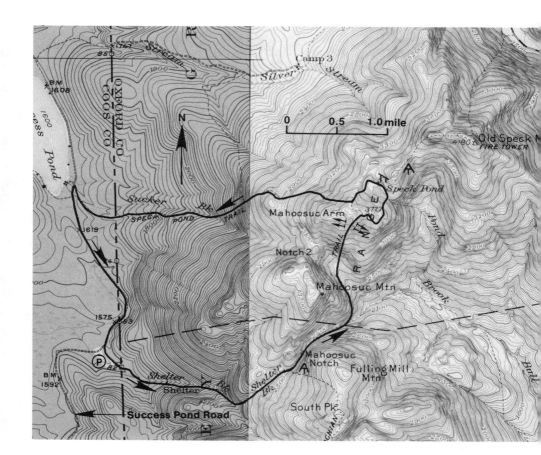

The climb in to Speck Pond via Mahoosuc Notch makes a long, rugged day hike or a leisurely paced overnighter through some of Maine's most interesting mountain terrain. This route follows the Appalachian Trail (AT) through the granite rubble of Mahoosuc Notch, the section of the trail that many hikers consider the most difficult. Speck Pond, your destination, is a serene, small body of water located in a 3500-foot-high basin, between Mahoosuc Arm and Old Speck Mountain. The traverse of the notch provides some of the most unusual, if demanding, hiking in eastern America. Fine views of the pond and its northerly neighbor, Old Speck, are seen on both the approach and return as you go over Mahoosuc Arm.

To reach the Notch Trail, take the Success Pond Road from the James River Company (formerly Brown Company) pulp yards in Berlin, New Hampshire. (For directions, see Hike 32). Approximately 11 miles from the paved road, watch for white trail markers to the right. A narrow, dirt road runs east here for about 0.1 mile to a parking space in a grassy clearing.

The Notch Trail crosses a shallow brook and follows a little-used tote road to the south-southeast. You shortly cross a second brook and reach a broad clearing with an old house. Passing a grove of aspens, you leave the road and make an abrupt *left* just beyond the clearing. Here the trail runs east-southeast and east up slight grades on an unused fire road bordered with great clusters of blackberry bushes. The path soon rejoins the brook on your left, which it recrosses in about ½ mile, continuing eastward.

The brook is crossed twice again as you walk eastward, finally following a small inlet to the left and north of a series of open barrens. The trail levels off on this height-of-land, meandering northeastward through a deciduous forest to a junction with the Appalachian Trail 2¼ miles from your starting point. (Note: The Appalachian Trail (AT) is known as the Mahoosuc Trail in this section and is referred to by that name on trail markers along the path.)

From the trail junction, head left and north on the Mahoosuc Trail (AT). You drop down immediately into the trench of the notch. The air temperature changes suddenly, often being 10 or 20 degrees cooler than on the trail you just left, however warm the day. Snow lingers here until well into summer. The route proceeds over huge slabs of rock that have fallen from the sides of Mahoosuc and Fulling Mill Mountains, and is marked by a series of white blazes. For more than 1 mile, you clamber to the northeast over and under this great jumble of rock. Use extra caution in this section; rock surfaces may be slippery, and the danger of losing your footing and dropping into a hole is constant. A small soft pack works well in the notch, as larger frame packs are very difficult to maneuver through the boulder caves and, in some places, may prove a real hindrance.

In the notch, the route gradually descends, joining a brook near the lower end. Emerging from the cleft between the mountains, you move away from the brook and left or northwestward, rising up the east side of Mahoosuc Mountain and then northward up Mahoosuc Arm. As you move onto the Arm, an old logging road is followed briefly, the trail then crossing a brook into a lumbered area. From here, you climb on increasingly stiff grades through balsam and red spruce, ascending sharply up over

Speck Pond

Mahoosuc Notch and Speck Pond Loop **127**

Trail junction, Mahoosuc Notch

the boulders and ledges which characterize the top of the Arm.

The views south from the bare summit of Mahoosuc Arm are excellent. Here, from your platform of folded, metamorphosed rock, you can see back down into the notch. Rock slides on Fulling Mill Mountain and open ledges on Mahoosuc Mountain mark the portals of the notch. To the north lies the rolling expanse of Old Speck. Slide Mountain and Riley Mountain are the two summits nearby to the east, and, behind them, rest the long, rangy summit of Sunday River Whitecap.

Head north and right on the Mahoosuc Trail toward Old Speck. You'll drop rapidly down to Speck Pond, approaching the pond from its south end. Follow the northeast shore of the pond around to Speck Pond Shelter. The shelter and several tent platforms provide overnight accommodations. Located right on the

shore, this site makes a very attractive overnight camp. Because of heavy use, particularly by "through hikers," the shelter is supervised by a caretaker during the peak months of June, July, and August. A small fee is charged for overnight stays. (Pack in your own gear and food.) The shelter area provides a pleasant spot to have your lunch if you are planning to hike out again the same day. (For overnighters, this is a good base camp from which to climb Old Speck via the west ridge above the pond.)

To return to Success Pond Road, take the Speck Pond Trail as it departs northwest from the shelter. You turn shortly, climbing very steeply southwest to the summit of the Arm. Look back for frequent superb views of the pond and Old Speck, which are particularly striking at late afternoon in good weather. In about ⅓ mile, you pass the

May Cutoff to the left. Stay *right* here, proceeding downward on the Speck Pond Trail to the west and southwest.

The descent runs first through tall groves of beautiful balsam, leveling off briefly on the north end of a ridge (2950 feet). Slabbing downward to the southwest, you descend through evergreens and mixed hardwoods, where open patches permit good views to the area west of Success Pond. The descent becomes gradually less steep, entering an area where you cross several logging roads. Keep a sharp lookout for trail blazes here, as it is easy to wander off the path. One mile above the road, the path joins the route of a prominent logging road, moving to the northwest and then around to the southwest. Bluets and painted trillium border the path, and moose footprints and droppings are frequently spotted.

In minutes, you join another logging right-of-way and emerge on a gravel road. Turn left here and follow this road south a short distance to where it intersects Success Pond Road. Continue south on Success Pond Road to the Notch Trail sign where you left your car (about 1½ miles).

Old Speck

Distance (round trip): 7¾ miles
Hiking time: 6 hours
Vertical rise: 2730 feet
Maps: USGS 15' Old Speck Mountain, Maine; USGS 15' Milan,
  New Hampshire

Maine's third highest mountain (after Katahdin and Sugarloaf) will give you something to sink your teeth into. Whether you're determined to head straight up, or to make the long traverse of the north ridge, Old Speck provides the king of hiking experience that lets you know you're in Maine. The mountain rises high over Grafton Notch and is reached via ME 26 from Bethel. Overnight camping is available on a first-come, first-served basis at Grafton Notch Shelter on the Appalachian Trail, about ½ mile east of the Old Speck trailhead.

The trail system on the mountain and in the notch has undergone some changes, and you should be aware that old maps may not have an accurate picture of available routes up the mountain. The Old Speck Trail, once known as the Fire Warden's Trail, now runs slightly north of the old route, and begins at a parking area on ME 26 a bit less than 3 miles north of Screw Auger Falls and about 12 miles northwest of Bethel. The old, badly eroded fire warden's route is no longer in use. The

Storm Clouds atop Old Speck

"new" Old Speck Trail includes parts of the former Cascade Brook Trail, the Eyebrow Trail, the Upper Ridge Link Trail, and the Skyline Trail. The route is clearly marked and there is a map of the route on a trailboard at the parking area. The Old Speck Trail is the current route of the Appalachian Trail.

From the north side of the parking area, the Old Speck Trail runs west nearly on the level, bears left at a fork where the Eyebrow Trail comes in from the right, and climbs easily in the direction of the summit. Heading south-southwest, you cross Cascade Brook. Several feeder brooks are soon passed. You turn around to the north, slabbing the ridge as the trail runs through the first of two north-south S-curves. Passing close to the lower cascades on your right, you proceed southwest again, then turn north through the second S and head west, rising quickly to the left of the cascades.

The upper reaches of the brook are followed to approximately the ¾-mile point where the trail turns sharply right, crosses the brook, and moves northward along ledges toward the Eyebrow. There are excellent views down the valley in this section.

To continue toward the summit, follow the Old Speck Trail through an ever-green grove north and northwest, then swing west up the ridge to the uneven timberline. At 1½ miles, open spaces provide views of the summit approximately 2¼ miles away. A long ridge walk takes you through forests of red spruce, over a series of hummocks and bare ledges.

At ¾ mile below the summit, the Link Trail down to the site of the old fire warden's cabin is passed. The Old Speck Trail dips into a final depression before rising sharply to a junction with the Mahoosuc Trail, which runs right to Speck Pond Shelter (see Hike 33). You turn left here and, passing the old Fire Warden's Trail on the left, arrive in about ¼ mile at the 4180-foot summit.

An observation tower on the summit is worth a careful climb, for the views run 360 degrees and are outstanding. You can look to the southwest directly down Mahoosuc Notch, framed by Mahoosuc and Fulling Mill Mountains. The twin peaks of Baldpate rise strikingly to the northeast; Dresser and Long Mountains are due east, with Slide Mountain and Sunday River Whitecap to the southeast. On a clear day, if you look beyond Baldpate, the mountains of the Rangeley region—particularly Saddleback—stand out. There is plenty of room on the wooded summit to stretch out or prepare lunch, and you may encounter a large, friendly rabbit with whom I've had several one-sided conversations.

The return trip is made by retracing your steps back to ME 26. Although technically possible, a return to the road via the old Fire Warden's Trail is not recommended.

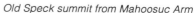

Old Speck summit from Mahoosuc Arm

35

Baldpate Mountain

Distance (round trip including Table Rock): 8½ miles
Hiking time: 6½ hours
Vertical rise: 2700 feet
Map: USGS 15' Old Speck Mountain

Grafton Notch remains a place to gladden the heart of civilization haters. It's a remote region, unspoiled and just enough out of the way to have escaped the tourist hordes and developers. Grafton Notch Road (ME 26) meanders through some beautiful farm country and between the mountains. There are some streams along here, too, which harbor their share of trout, and moose are seen often. In short, the notch provides some robust hiking in a very attractive western Maine setting.

The Appalachian Trail (AT), the route for this hike, ascends Baldpate from ME 26 in Grafton Notch opposite the parking area for Old Speck (Hike 34). The route has been relocated in recent years, and shelter access changed to eliminate wear on older sections of the trail. The new section of the AT begins on the east side of the road and runs east-northeast across a grassy marsh area and into a grove of spruce and hardwoods. The newly constructed loop to Table Rock is passed on the right in a few minutes. Keep on the main trail and save the side trip to Table Rock for the trip back.

Continuing upward on the white-blazed AT, you shortly reach one of the feeder brooks that spills into the Bear

River. At approximately ½ mile from the road, blue-blazed trails depart left to the lean-to. This shelter offers limited accommodation and at the height of the season may be fully used, so packing a tent along may be advisable if you plan to camp.

The route broadens above the shelter, meandering southeast and northeast through mixed growth, reaching the Table Rock Trail at just under 1 mile. The Table Rock Trail leads to the right almost due south, and takes you to some of the finest views in the notch. This side trail rises easily southward through slender hardwoods, crosses a rivulet, and then climbs somewhat more steeply up a dome to the Table. This short detour is worth the walk, for views of old Speck, Sunday River Whitecap, and Puzzle Mountain (way down the Bear River Valley) are truly excellent. The distance from the AT to the Table and back is under 1 mile.

Back at the trail junction, you continue rightward up Baldpate and, crossing a brook, follow the trail as it rises to the east through bushes which nearly obscure the path in midsummer. The going here may be wet. This is also prime country for moose-spotting. The

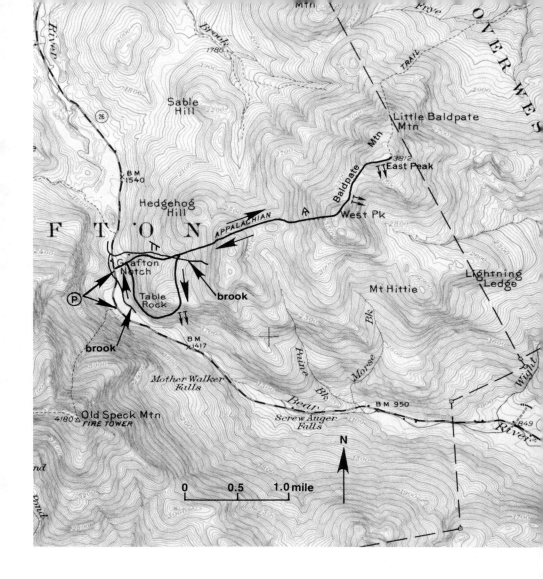

enormous animals, more shy now that they are being hunted in Maine again after a 30-year hiatus, like the succulent young browse that characterizes this section of the trail.

At about 2 miles above the road, the trail runs more to the east and southeast as it climbs a low knob. The summit of the West Peak is reached at 3 miles from the trailhead. Views to the northwest

open up as you cross the west summit and continue northeastward along a ridge. You drop down to a depression, cross a brook, and begin the steady ascent of Baldpate's east peak. There are open spots here with good views. Moving eastward still, you climb over open ledges and reach the east peak at a bit more than 3¾ miles.

The outlook makes the long trudge in

Baldpate—west and east peaks

from the road seem trifling. You can look northward over Little Baldpate and Surplus Mountains, which create a watershed for eastward-running Frye Brook. The bare summit of Sunday River Whitecap, due south over Mount Hittie, is visible, as are Dresser and Long Mountains in an arc to the southeast. Black Mountain and Gregg Mountain are the two low summits immediately to the east-northeast. Old Speck looms to the southwest.

The trip back to the road is made by retracing your steps. If you did not make the side trip to Table Rock on the ascent, it can be made on your way down. Turn left on the Table Rock side trail. After visiting the Table, follow the blue-blazed loop trail which ascends the steep terrain beneath the Table and rejoins the AT just east of the road.

Mount Desert Island–
Acadia National Park

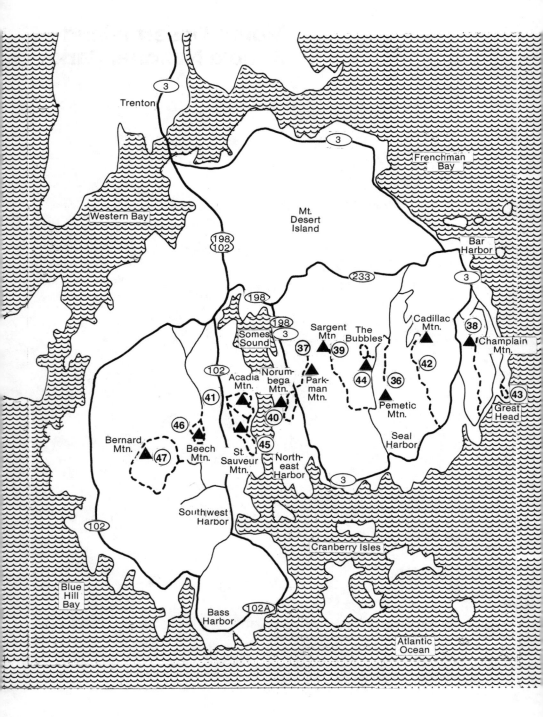

Trenton
③

Western Bay

Mt.
Desert
Island

Frenchman
Bay

Bar
Harbor

③

Somes
Sound

Sargent
Mtn

The
Bubbles

Cadillac
Mtn.

38

Champlain
Mtn.

37

39

42

Acadia
Mtn.

Norum-
bega
Mtn.

Park-
man
Mtn.

44

36

43

41

40

Pemetic
Mtn.

Great
Head

46

45

Bernard
Mtn.

Beech
Mtn.

St.
Sauveur
Mtn.

North-
east
Harbor

Seal
Harbor

47

Southwest
Harbor

Cranberry Isles

Blue
Hill
Bay

Bass
Harbor

Atlantic
Ocean

102A

102

102

198
102

198

198

233

③

③

③

③

INTRODUCTION

Mount Desert is the largest coastal island in Maine. Its kidney-shaped land mass lies off Trenton at the Head of Frenchman Bay, east of Blue Hill and west of Schoodic Point. A heavily glaciated, mountainous island, Mount Desert makes a spectacular destination for the hiker. Clearly marked, highly attractive trails ascend to dozens of well-placed summits scattered all over the island. Shore walks and strolls through small villages provide pleasant walking, too. The natural beauty of Mount Desert defies easy description, but to say that it has few equals anywhere in America isn't hyperbole. You will have to see for yourself, and the trail descriptions in this section provide a thorough introduction to the best of Mount Desert Island.

The lands of Acadia National Park are at the core of Mount Desert's natural attractiveness. The park is a sort of enclave within the larger boundaries of the island, and contains all of the walks in this section. Some of the trails are reached only by the park service road which may be entered at Hulls Cove in the north or at other points on the island. An entrance fee must be paid to use this road and other park facilities. Other hikes on the island are reached on toll-free state roads (see each hike description for access directions). Acadia also features campgrounds, picnic areas, boat-launch ramps, and beaches. A complete guide to park facilities may be found at the Hulls Cove entrance. Russell Butcher's *Guide to Acadia National Park*, available in local stores, is must reading.

The best time to visit Mount Desert is during the months of October through May. High summer tends to be increasingly crowded, and the island's narrow roads fill up with that quintessential American phenomenon, the motorized sightseer. You won't see this person on the trails, for he or she never gets far from an automobile. They do, however, make it harder to get to that trailhead you're in search of. If you visit Acadia in the off-season, you'll find nary a person in the woods and that serene beauty for which Acadia is famous won't be overrun with the motorbound visitors. There are plenty of accommodations in the Ellsworth–Mount Desert region. Indeed, they are too plentiful, and their increasing numbers draw more congestion each year. Park service officials are urging local merchants not to overbuild, but, rather, to accommodate more people in the off-seasons. We concur in this advice, and you can do your part in preventing overuse by visiting from after Columbus Day up until Memorial Day.

Mount Desert and Acadia offer some fine terrain for the winter snow-shoer or cross-country skier. The carriage roads are ideal for ski touring, and portions of most of the walks in this section can be showshoed in season. The summits are often icy and blown free of snow in winter, so good boots and instep crampons (available at most mountaineering stores) are advisable. Don't let winter drive you away, though; it's a spectacularly pretty time of year on the island.

Bicyclists will enjoy Acadia, too, as many of the carriage roads make excellent bike routes, and the loop around Eagle Lake has been specially graded for cycling. The 43 miles of carriage roads are not open to motorized vehicles, so the cyclist can enjoy the tranquility he or she craves.

For further information, write: Superintendent, Acadia National Park, Bar Harbor, ME 04609. If you plan to camp in Acadia, write well in advance for reservations.

Pemetic Mountain

Distance (round trip): 2¼ miles
Hiking time: 2 hours
Vertical rise: 950 feet
Maps: USGS Acadia National Park and Vicinity; AMC Map of
  Mount Desert Island

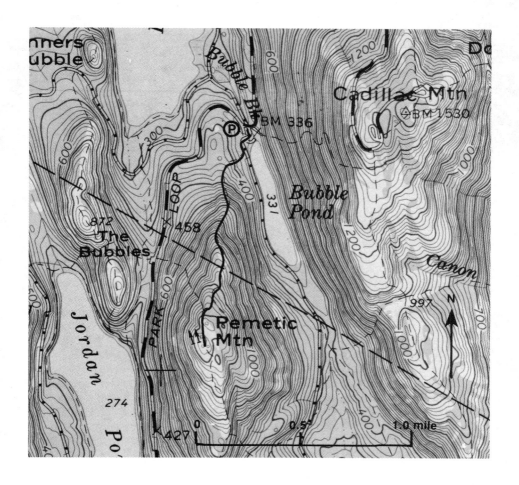

Morning mist on Pemetic Mountain

Rising nearly in the center of Mount Desert's "eastern half," Pemetic Mountain provides some excellent views east toward Cadillac and west to Sargent Mountain, and to the parklands to the north on Eagle Lake. A bit out of the way and less frequented than some climbs on the island, Pemetic offers you exceptional rewards as a first, short hike.

The Pemetic Mountain Trail, which runs the full length of the ridge and terminates at ME 3 in Seal Harbor, begins at the north end of Bubble Pond. To reach Bubble Pond, go south on the park service road which leaves ME 3 at park headquarters above Hulls Cove (northwest of Bar Harbor). Park your car in the area provided at the north shore of the pond (off the park service road).

The name Pemetic derives from local Native American parlance, meaning simply a range of hills. From the north end of the pond, you head southwesterly, traveling along the west shore briefly, passing through cedar groves, then turning due west, and crossing over one of the many carriage roads which traverse the island.

Past the road, you swing southwest again, walking easily through a second cedar grove at ⅓ mile. Passing through a range of some fine, tall firs, you begin to climb more steadily, moving south-southwesterly now toward the summit. This area is densely grown with evergreens and provides some truly pleasant walking. It's a movie set kind of forest. At

⅔ mile, the trail runs more southerly, passing a boulder-strewn way and along the ledges on the east side of the mountain. There is a good view of Cadillac Mountain to the left as you walk this section.

Turning more westerly, the trail soon brings you to a second ledgy area, where outlooks to the north appear. On clear days, when weather isn't "making" in the valleys, good views of Eagle Lake are yours here. Continuing in the same direction, the second, more open, summit will be reached in about ⅛ mile.

From the summit, the striking, bare ridge to the west is Penobscot and Sargent Mountains. Almost due north of the Pemetic summit, you can see the full length of Eagle Lake, while to the east and northeast is the long rise of Cadillac Mountain. The open ledges on which you are standing are extensive and make for interesting exploring. There are several good spots on the ledges to rest and have lunch before heading down.

In descending to Bubble Pond on your return, watch the trail carefully. The dense growth makes it easy to take a wrong turn as you head down. Cairns and red blazes help mark the trail. A general northeast course cannot fail to bring you to the road if the trail should be lost.

37

Parkman Mountain and Bald Peak

Distance (round trip): 2½ miles
Hiking time: 2 hours
Vertical rise: 700 feet
Maps: USGS Acadia National Park and Vicinity; AMC Map of
  Mount Desert Island

On a sunny, summer day at the height of the season, when many of Mount Desert's trails may have more hikers on them than you care to contend with, two low summits northeast of the Hadlock ponds make an excellent hike. Parkman Mountain and Bald Peak form the west leg of a triangle with Penobscot and Sargent Mountains, and furnish five vantage points over lands to the north and west of the island. These two mountains are really no more than hills, but the easy hike into both provides pleasant walking over varied terrain, and you're likely to have the summits pretty much to yourself.

To reach the trailhead, drive west from Bar Harbor on ME 233 or east from Somesville on ME 198. At the junction of the two roads, continue south on ME 198 for about 3 miles, watching for the parking lot by the trailhead on the east side of the road. You may also reach this spot by driving north on ME 198 from Northeast Harbor.

A rough trail runs almost directly up Parkman, but it is hard to find in places and is poorly marked. A more reliable route begins at the northeast corner of the parking area on a short link to a carriage road. Take this link to the carriage road and turn right, walking uphill to the southeast, arriving in a few minutes at a junction. Bear sharply *left* at the junction, continuing upward on another unpaved road through a long S-curve. At the top of the curve, about ¼ mile above, watch for trail signs on the left.

You turn off the road at the trail signs and walk northwest over a ledgy shelf through groves of jack pines. The trail recrosses the road at the top of the rise and, turning more northward, enters the woods again. Your route here lies over more sandy ledge amid thin, mixed growth and curves gradually around to the east. The trail shortly passes through a grove of cedars, and levels off briefly, running east-northeast. Early views of Bald Peak's summit may be had here. The trail is marked with small cairns and paint blazes.

Approximately ⅔ mile from the parking area, a more pronounced scramble up the rocks begins, with occasional views to the north opening up. You drop briefly into a depression and then climb briskly eastward on a series of bare ledges. Excellent views of both Upper and Lower Hadlock Ponds emerge in this section. In minutes, you slab east-

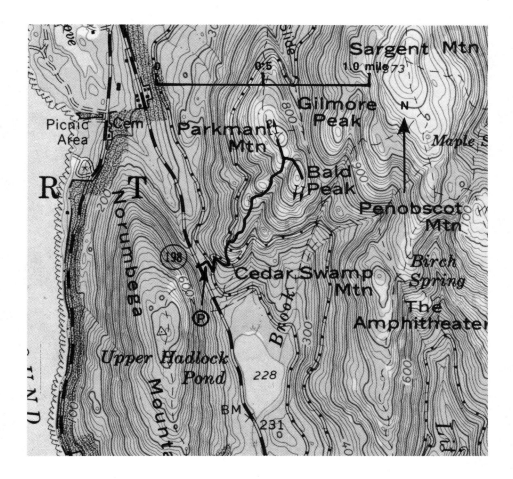

northeast over a knob and above a shallow ravine to your right. The ridge, with Parkman Mountain to the left and Bald Peak to the right, lies just above with fine outlooks to the northwest and west as you ascend.

At the top of the ridge, a link trail runs south-southeast to Bald Peak. Turn right here, dropping down into a wooded cleft between the two summits. The link rises quickly and, in ¼ mile, you crest the granite summit of aptly named Bald Peak. Excellent views of the Hadlock

Ponds and the lowlands down the valley to Northeast Harbor are to your south here. Greening Island and the open Atlantic lie to the south-southwest. Immediately to the west over the arm of land you have just climbed, you will see the north-south expanse of Norumbega Mountain (see Hike 40). Penobscot and Cedar Swamp Mountains are to the east and southeast.

To reach Parkman Mountain, retrace your steps to the ridgetop trail junction, then turn right and northward on the trail

Parkman Mountain and Bald Peak

over the ledges. You'll arrive on Parkman's 940-foot summit in moments. From this totally bare mound of rock, you have a superb vantage point over the northern reaches of Somes Sound and, beyond Somesville, Western Bay. On clear days, you may also see Blue Hill, Bald Mountain, and Mount Waldo on the mainland to the west. The low summit of Acadia Mountain is visible over the northern flanks of Norumbega Mountain to the immediate west. Sargent and Penobscot Mountains make up the bright stone ridge across the ravine to the east.

Although Parkman and Bald are not high by the standard of many mountains in Maine, they can be very windy. Winds from the south seem to accelerate as they come up the valley from the ocean and may often reach gale velocity on days when it is warm and calm at roadside.

To regain the road, head down on the Parkman Mountain trail by which you ascended, using caution not to lose the trail where it crosses the carriage road.

Gorham and Champlain Mountains

Distance (round trip): 6 miles
Hiking time: 4 hours
Vertical rise: 1200 feet
Maps: USGS 7½' Seal Harbor; USGS Acadia National Park
  and Vicinity; AMC Map of Mount Desert Island

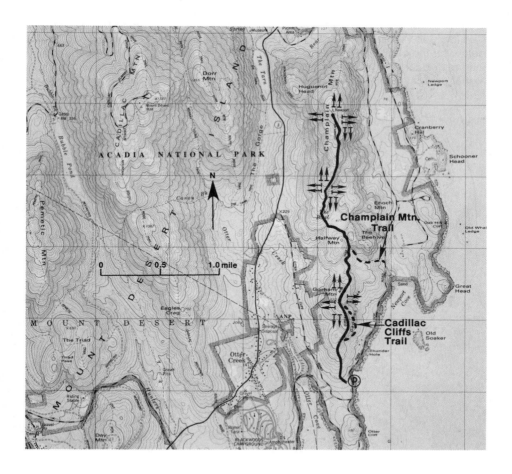

Together, Gorham and Champlain Mountains form the easternmost north-south ridge on Mount Desert Island. Because their summits look immediately down on a splendid coastline, the ridge walk is one of the best on the island. The walk described here is over both peaks, from south to north, and returning.

Leave your car at the Monument Cove parking lot (indicated by a "Gorham Mt. Trail" sign) on Ocean Drive about 1 mile south of Sand Beach and 1 mile north of Otter Cliffs. Take the Gorham Mountain Trail, which starts on the west side of the road, opposite the cove. Watch for the marker. You climb easily over open ledges for about ⅓ mile, passing the Cadillac Cliffs Loop Trail on the right. (A detour for the cliffs may be taken; the loop rejoins the main trail about ⅓ mile higher up.)

Your walk above the cliffs continues, rising very slightly over open ledges with good views, passes the other end of the Cliffs Loop at about ⅔ mile, and proceeds north to the open summit at just under 1 mile. Superb north-to-south views of the island's southeast coast are to be had here.

Over the summit, you descend for ⅓ mile to a connection with the Champlain Mountain Trail. Turn northwest (left) at this junction. You ascend the south ridge of Champlain gradually, proceeding around the Bowl (a mountain tarn), which is on your right, then turn north on the open ridge with more excellent views of the ocean to the east. The summit of Champlain is reached after slightly less than 3 miles of hiking from the trailhead.

From the summit, you'll see Huguenot Head tumble northwest toward Dorr and

Otter Cliff

Cadillac Mountains. The community of Bar Harbor is north-northeast from your vantage point, and Bar, Sheep Porcupine, Burnt Porcupine, and Long Porcupine Islands stand off the harbor. You will see a point of land to the southeast, above Newport Cove, which is Great Head. The long stretch of water above Bar Harbor is Frenchman Bay.

Located on this great bay, Mount Desert Island has played an intimate role in Maine's coastal history. There are signs of habitation on the island prior to 4000 B.C. The island was a favorite summer home of the Passamaquoddy and Penobscot tribes of the Abenaki nation prior to the Colonial period. The Native Americans wintered at their tribal homes near Orono, Maine, paddling to the island in birchbark canoes in the warm months to fish and gather provisions.

To return via your ascent route, simply turn around on the Champlain summit and head back along the ridge the way you came. Monument Cove, your starting point, lies due south.

Penobscot and Sargent Mountains

Distance (round trip): 5 miles
Hiking time: 3½ hours
Vertical rise: 1150 feet
Maps: USGS Acadia National Park and Vicinity; AMC Map of
  Mount Desert Island

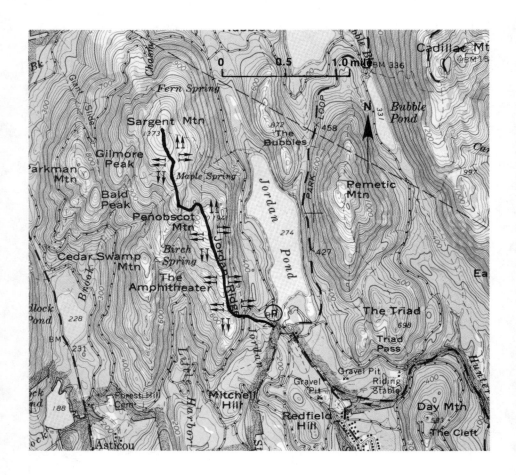

Penobscot Mountain over Long Pond

Penobscot and Sargent Mountains form the high ridge that runs down to the west side of Jordan Pond. Leave your car at the new Jordan Pond House, a popular eating place just north of Seal Harbor on the park service road. The trail begins from the rear of the house. Watch for an arrow, indicating the trail to the west.

After a short walk from the house, you cross the carriage road and bear slightly to the right over a footbridge spanning Jordan Stream. Follow signs for the Penobscot Mountain Trail. You travel west and northwest, rising very gradually for the first ⅓ mile. The trail then climbs more rapidly for a while, levels off briefly, descends to cross another brook, and turns left below a wall of granite boulders.

Slabbing left up the wall, you cross a second carriage road and resume the steep northwest pitch up the ridge. The climb becomes very interesting here, and you will traverse several rock ledges that are nearly perpendicular. *Caution is required.* Be very careful not to dislodge loose rock which could fall on a climber below. The trail here follows a series of switchbacks, with some straight vertical climbing.

After maneuvering up through a narrow crack and around another switchback, you emerge onto a ledge (right) with excellent views down to Jordan Pond and across the water to Pemetic Mountain. The two round peaks known as the Bubbles are to the left at the far end of the pond. Continue west now, climbing through a wooded area to an open ledge at the peak of the south ridge. You turn abruptly right here and head north along the ridge toward the Penobscot summit.

The views are very good on the ridge (you can see almost full circle, from northeast to northwest) and get progressively better as you near the top. The trail meanders over the bare ridge, passing several false summits, and reaches the true summit, directly opposite Pemetic, at 1½ miles.

The summit of Sargent Mountain is just under 1 mile north. Below you to the northwest is Sargent Pond, a tiny alpine lake. To reach the pond, take the Sargent Pond Trail from the summit of Penobscot. The descent to the pond is quickly made over ledgy terrain. The South Ridge Trail is well marked and leads from the pond directly in ¾ mile to the top of Sargent. Allow at least an additional ½ hour to get over to Sargent.

Looking south from either peak, you will quickly come to appreciate why climbing on Mount Desert Island is unique. For besides the excellent mountain views to the west, north, and east, there are superb views of the Atlantic to the south. The point of land to the southeast is Seal Harbor, and out beyond are the islands which lie off Mount Desert's southern shores. The largest, slightly to the left, is Great Cranberry Island. To the northeast lie Little Cranberry and Baker Islands. The three smaller islands closer to the shore are, left to right, Sutton, Bear, and Greening. Farther out, Little Duck and Great Duck may be visible if the weather is exceptionally clear. Having surveyed the peaks and islands, head down to the Jordan Pond House via the long, splendid walk south on the Penobscot Trail.

Although Penobscot and Sargent are low summits by the standard of Maine's major mountains, you should travel prepared. As on Cadillac and Champlain, these ridges are open to wind and weather from all directions and offer little shelter. Be sure to carry extra clothing in case of sudden changes in the weather.

Norumbega Mountain

Distance (around loop): 2¾ miles
Hiking time: 2 hours
Vertical rise: 600 feet
Maps: USGS Acadia National Park and Vicinity; AMC Map of
*   Mount Desert Island*

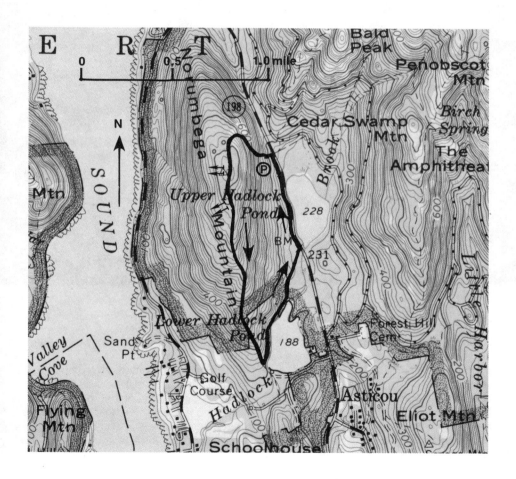

Shore Trail on Mount Desert Island

Physically, Mount Desert Island is a heart-shaped land mass, divided in the middle by the fjordlike Somes Sound, and peppered with bare summits rising dramatically from the sea. Norumbega Mountain is a low summit that forms the eastern wall of the sound and provides nearly as much good hiking as many of its higher neighbors on the mainland.

The views, as one would expect, are first class.

On its eastern perimeter, Norumbega lies side by side with Upper and Lower Hadlock Ponds. The summit, besides monitoring the length of the sound, looks south to the lowlands of Southwest Harbor and Tremont. Norumbega also forms the left leg of a horseshoe-shaped series of peaks whose eastern border consists of Sargent and Penobscot Mountains. The mountain was formerly known as Brown's Mountain after John Brown, an early settler who owned a major plot of land north of the rise.

To reach the mountain from the junction of ME 198 and ME 233, take ME 198 south along the eastern edge of Somes Sound. At 2.8 miles from the junction watch for a parking area on the west side of the road, just above Upper Hadlock Pond.

From the parking area, you walk westward on the Norumbega Mountain Trail. Ascending steeply, you turn northwestward—away from the summit—slab the ridge, and then turn south at about ⅓ mile. The climb continues southward, rising over more open granite ledges (with scattered views) and reaches the summit at ⅔ mile. The summit is wooded, but allows fine open views to the west and up the sound. The mountains across the water are Saint Sauveur and Acadia. Farther back are Bernard, Mansell, and Beach Mountains, ranging left to right, one almost behind the other. Rest awhile here and soak it all up.

There are blueberry bushes on the north ridge, and if you climb in mid-summer you can well gather the mak-ings of a pie before leaving the summit. Underway again, continue down the trail to the south. The walk through mixed fir, pine, and spruce straddles the south ridge. The trail descends easily and, in about 1⅔ miles from the parking lot, reaches the west shore of Lower Hadlock Pond. You turn sharply north-east here, following the *west* shore of the pond. *Keeping west* of the pond and its northern brook, you reach Route 198 at 2¼ miles. Turn left (north) on the road which takes you back to your staring point, not quite ¾ mile away.

Acadia Mountain Loop

Distance (around loop): 2½ miles
Hiking time: 1½ hours
Vertical rise: 500 feet
Maps: USGS 7½' Southwest Harbor; USGS Acadia National
  Park and Vicinity; AMC Map of Mount Desert Island

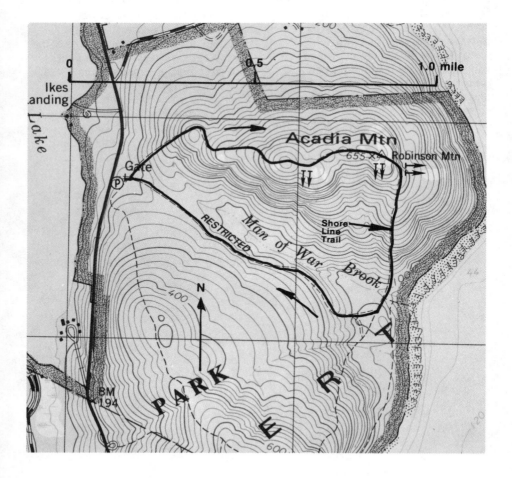

Acadia Mountain is one of the attractive, low summits that border Somes Sound on the western half of Mount Desert Island. The sound, which many consider the only real coastal fjord in eastern America (because the mountains plunge right down to the sea here), rolls south to the sea directly under Acadia's east peak. You'll be able to approach the sound on the lower reaches of this hike where the trail crosses Man o' War Brook. The area, besides being a supremely attractive hiking ground, has many historic associations. Nearby Saint Sauveur Mountain bears the name of the early French colony on the island, founded in 1613. The colony was destroyed in a matter of weeks by marauding English coastal patrols. The English men-of-war found the deep waters of the sound a good place to drop anchor close to shore. Fresh water from Man o' War Brook and fish and game from the area replenished the larders of the English fighting ships.

The west-to-east traverse of Acadia Mountain begins on ME 102, 3 miles south of Somesville and 3 miles north of Southwest Harbor. A large parking area on the west side of the road above Echo Lake is situated opposite the trailhead. The trail runs east over a bluff and into the woods. Quickly ascending a series of ledges, you walk east-southeast through groves of jack pines and birches, which are surrounded by blueberry bushes.

You shortly reach a junction, and turn north and left through a slump over-grown with rhodora, thence climbing slightly over several ledgy ribs. In moments you cross gravel Robinson Road, reenter the woods, and directly ascend a low ledge. The trail now rises more steeply north-northeastward to a second ledgy area where views to the west begin to open up. You curve around to the east-southeast over the attractive exposed granite, passing through a shady depression filled with thickly grown pine and Indian pipes. Early views of the south end of the sound may be seen here and in a few more minutes you reach Acadia's west summit, which has spectacular views to the south, but is wooded on its north side. (A short side trail leads to a bald spot with good views on the north lip of the knob.) Although you'll be pleased with what you see from this spot, there are even better views from the east peak. To get there, simply walk eastward through a depression grown up with stunted oak and rhodora, emerging on the east summit in a few minutes.

Acadia's east knob provides a splendid outlook on Somes Sound and the offshore islands to the south. Beautiful Valley Cove is below to the near south, and above it to the right lies Saint Sauveur Mountain. Flying Mountain is the low hill that juts out into the water beyond the cove. Across the water, the hulk of Norumbega Mountain runs north and south. The peak to the west with the prominent tower is Beech Mountain. A number of large sailing craft are usually moored around the cove in fair weather. The prospect from this side of Acadia is profoundly beautiful, and you'll want to allow time to sit on the rocks here, enjoying it all.

To descend to Man o' War Brook, head east of the summit over rolling ledges and down into groves of red oak. The trail turns south and makes its way down over several ledges in switchbacks that are moderately steep. At ½ mile below the east peak, you enter a cedar grove and cross the brook. A link trail to the left leads 100 yards to the shoreline. Continue south on the main trail, turning southwest and right at a trail junction. You next cross a field and

Acadia Mountain (right) and Norumbega Mountain over Somes Sound

reach the end of Robinson Road. Follow the road northwest as it rises gently, passing very attractive groves of cedar. There are periodic views of the bare ledges of Acadia's west peak before you enter the woods here.

Continue along the road to the northwest for about ½ mile, watching for trail signs at the crossing. Turn left and west at the point where you crossed the road originally, and retrace your steps back to ME 102 in another ¼ mile.

Cadillac Mountain

Distance (round trip): 7 miles
Hiking time: 4½ hours
Vertical rise: 1230 feet
Maps: USGS Acadia National Park and Vicinity; AMC Map of
*   Mount Desert Island*

Cadillac Mountain, Mount Desert's highest summit, broods over the eastern half of the island, its great 5-mile-long bulk visible from almost anywhere on the land or water around it. The mountain, named after Antoine Cadillac, who was given the island by Louis XIV in 1688, offers what is perhaps the best extended walk along open heights on the island. The walk culminates in superb views over the entire island, Frenchman Bay, and the Atlantic.

To ascend Cadillac, drive south from Bar Harbor on Route 3. Watch for trail signs on the north side of the road nearly opposite the entrance to Black Woods Campground. There is ample room to park cars on the shoulder of the road. From the road, the trail immediately enters thick woods, running north and northwest on a gradual rise through close-grown balsam, white pine, and cedar. The ground cover has been eroded in many places, and the distinctive pink granite of the island frequently protrudes.

You walk through scattered boulders and rock slabs, arriving at a junction with the loop to Eagle Crag on the right in 1 mile. Eagle Crag offers much the same views as the main trail. Keep left

here and stay on the main trail under the rock outcrops, climbing northwestward to the first open ledges with views to the southwest. At just over 1½ miles from the road, the trail wanders through birch and groves of jack pine into open, 180-degree views to the south. On summer days, a great deal of sailing activity around the islands to the south may be seen from here.

The trail continues over open ledges and through occasional scrub along the north-south rib of the mountain. Interesting dikes of metamorphosed shale are seen here and there in the rock, and the summit appears ahead to the right. You may also look east, taking in the whole range of Gorham and Champlain Mountains, including the tiny mountain tarn known as the Bowl. About 1 mile below the summit, the route descends into a gully, passing a pretty bog to the left and crossing the Canon Brook Trail.

For the remainder of the route below the summit, you walk completely in the open, and all vegetation ceases. Winds in this area can be uncomfortable in rough weather. Continuing north-northeast across the open slab, the trail loops to the edge of the road then runs through a wooded area to the summit

Cadillac, Dorr, and Champlain Mountains from Cadillac South Trail

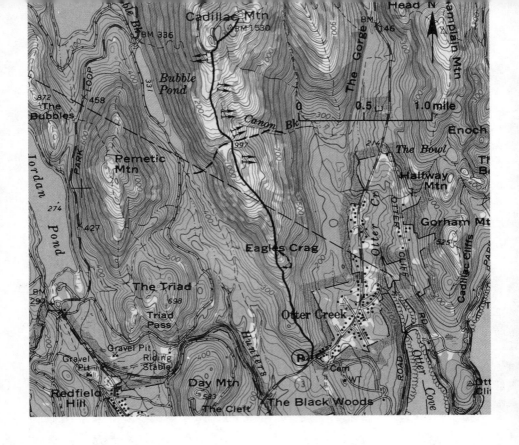

over short, easy grades. In a few minutes, you pass the true summit to the left behind the service building and emerge at the summit parking area. The open ledges with the best views lie a short walk to the east.

Cadillac's summit, being highest on the island, offers fine views in all directions. You'll see Dorr Mountain rising in the immediate foreground to the east. Behind it, the long ridge of Champlain Mountain, named after the island's discoverer, stands between Dorr and the sea. The islands of Bar Harbor and Frenchman Bay are to the northeast. Schoodic Point, also a part of Acadia National Park, lies far across the bay to the east. Pemetic, Penobscot, and

Sargent Mountains constitute the most imposing summits to the west, and are best seen in their entirety from the summit's west parking area.

From up here, it isn't hard to see why Mount Desert became such a hotly contested prize among the early colonial settlers. Discovered and first colonized by the French, the island later passed into British hands before being taken by the American Colonials. Its abundant excellent harbors, game, and notable water supplies made it a prize worth contesting.

To return to your car at Black Woods, retrace your route downward. The walk from the 1500-foot summit to ME 3 can be done in less than 2 hours.

Sand Beach and Great Head

Distance (round trip): 2 miles
Hiking time: 1½ hours
Vertical rise: 200 feet
*Maps: USGS 7½' Seal Harbor; USGS Acadia National Park
   and Vicinity; AMC Map of Mount Desert Island*

One of the most attractive stretches of shoreline on Mount Desert Island, Sand Beach and Great Head provide the walker with an easy route through varied, always beautiful terrain. The Head itself gives the hiker access to what are probably the best shoreline views on the east side of the island across the water to the Schoodic Peninsula. And, since the elevation gains on this route are minor, it's a good walk with youngsters or as an unde-manding stroll on a day when you'd like to mosey along the shore, avoiding the steeper climbs of Mount Desert's higher summits.

From Bar Harbor, head south on ME 3, reaching a fork in the road about 1 mile from the center of town. Keep to the left here on Schooner Head Road. Stay on this road for about 3 miles, making no turns, until it terminates at a barrier. Turn around here and park off the road anywhere near the trailhead, which is marked by a wooden pillar about 200 yards before the road end.

This walk makes a loop past Sand Beach and offers a shorter return over the inland ledges of the Head, or a longer walk along the perimeter of the Head, rejoining the shorter loop on the return. Both walks are undemanding and, except for a brief scramble up the ledges, require little climbing.

Begin by walking south on the trail through white birch, steeplebush, and spruce. The route lies over a broad woods road now turned grassy and well shaded. In a few hundred yards, you will pass the return leg of the path coming in on your left. Proceed straight ahead, and reach the bluffs over Sand Beach in ½ mile. Spectacular views over the beach and up to the Beehive, a rounded granitic mountain, open up to the west. You may wish to descend to the beach via a pathway now and explore the shore and the pretty freshwater lagoon behind it. Herons, ducks, and other shorebirds are often seen, particularly in early morning. The beach itself is a fine expanse of yellow sand which caps Newport Cove. Visit here in early or late season if you can. In high summer, the crowds descend.

Opposite the point where the side trail descends to the beach, the shorter of the two loops zigzags directly up a ledge marked with red blazes. If you wish to return this way, head up the ledge and arrive at a bare summit with superb views to the east and back to the

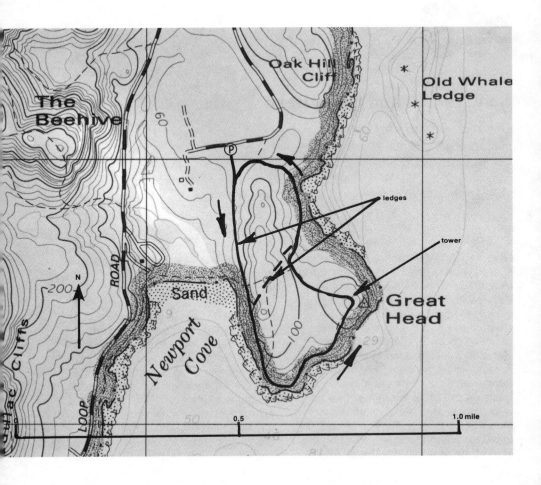

west over the Beehive and Champlain Mountain. The route then descends from the ledges and loops back on a well-marked trail to the junction mentioned earlier.

To reach Great Head, continue south and southeast, gradually rounding the end of the peninsula over mossy ground and rising and falling through aspen and birch. Following the red blazes and, later, cairns, you arrive shortly at the ruined stone tower of Great Head's 145-foot precipitous drop to the broad

Atlantic. You can see in all directions here: back to the mountains of the island, southeast to the open ocean, to the east across Frenchman Bay to the Schoodic region, and northeast to the mountains of the mainland. The tiny island with the squarish building is Egg Rock lighthouse, a beacon on the considerable water traffic which moves up and down the bay. Around to the southwest are the high, dark ledges forming Otter Cliffs. From here, you can also see Champlain Mountain and the

Beehive again, along whose summit ridges there are excellent, long, north-south day hikes (see Hike 38).

To return, leave the tower site and walk northwest, descending soon to a boggy area over more ledge. Scattered alders, bracken fern, and occasional spruce line the path as you move within earshot of the shore. Just beyond a thick stand of young birch where the ground is carpeted with bunchberry, Canada mayflower, moss, and lichen, you join the shorter of the two loop trails as it comes in on your left. Continuing northwest over easy grades, the trail broadens and becomes less stony. Reaching a height-of-land in a small clearing, you descend slightly, curving more westerly, and soon reach the main trail on which you began the walk. Bear right and north here, and you'll gain the paved road and your parking place in just a few minutes.

This walk can also be done in milder winters when there is likely to be little snow cover on the island. Good hiking boots should always be worn in winter or during inclement weather, as the frequent ledge-walking on this hike can be slippery.

Lower Frenchman Bay from Great Head

The Bubbles

Distance (round trip): 3½ miles
Hiking time: 2 hours
Vertical rise: 800 feet
Maps: USGS Acadia National Park and Vicinity; AMC Map of
Mount Desert Island

The Bubbles are two 800-foot mounds of pink granite which dominate the northern end of Jordan Pond in the east-central portion of Mount Desert Island. The two sister mountains form a striking profile that at first may discourage the hiker with no technical climbing experience. In fact, these two very rocky peaks require no special mountaineering skills and are readily accessible to the average hiker. The Bubbles not only offer a challenging outing for the hiker, but they are an elegant platform in the midst of Acadia National Park for viewing nearly all of the major summits that surround it.

This hike is directly reached by driving ME 3 east from Ellsworth to the north end of Mount Desert Island and turning onto the park service road at the Hulls Cove entrance. An information center is just inside this entrance, and directions and park maps can be asked for here if you need them. Proceed south on the park service road to the Bubble Rock Parking Area north of Jordan Pond. This spot is also known as the "Bubble-Pemetic" parking area, and shouldn't be confused with the "Bubbles" parking lot still another half mile further south.

The walk begins to the west from the

parking area, rising up through closely grown beech, birch, and striped maple. You reach a junction in less then ⅛ mile and cross the Jordan Pond Carry Trail. From here, continue straight on up an old tote road which bears gradually to the left, over several water bars, arriving shortly at another junction. Trails lead from this junction to both of the Bubble summits.

Bear left and ascend the trail to the South Bubble. The climb is brisk up through young beech and birch. With Pemetic Mountain off to your left, you keep left at the junction with the trail from Jordan Pond. Views to the North Bubble begin to open up behind you now. At just under 800 feet, the summit of the South Bubble is an open expanse of glacier-scarred granite, onto which you soon emerge after a final march amid scraggly birch and alder.

Potassium feldspar accounts for the characteristic pink glow of Mount Desert's coarse granite hills. The igneous stone was formed approximately 350 million years ago and has been glacially scoured several times since, most recently 18,000 to 11,000 years ago. The Laurentide ice sheet, the most recent of the glacial waves to come down from the northwest over New England, was roughly 2000 feet thick as it built up and then slid over this range. One effect of the ice was the pleasing, rounded shape of the mountains in this area, further aided by subsequent weathering. As the ice moved through any depressions, it ground and chiseled them until they became the valleys that run characteristically north and south on Mount Desert.

The north and northwest sides of most mountains in Acadia bear glacial scars from the grinding, rolling action of stone and sand carried along by glacial ice. As the ice moved over these ranges, the mobile sand and stone were dragged under tremendous pressure across existing formations. Those mountain's southern and southeastern sides of Mount Desert show rather sheer, precipitous faces due to the circular motion of glacially carried rock known as "plucking." Both of the Bubbles exhibit these phenomena.

Jordan and Great Ponds give you a sense of how efficient glacial action could be at scraping off deposits and carrying them away. The ponds are quite deep from the scouring and transporting action of sheet ice. The material dredged from these spots by the action of the ice was deposited further down at the south ends of the valleys. The action of the great ice sheets also transported large boulders, called glacial erratics, from distances as far away as 20 miles. One of the most prominent of these erratics can be seen just a few yards south of the South Bubble summit.

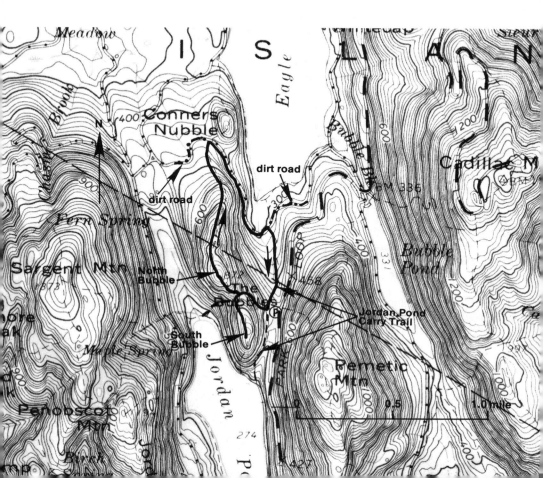

North Bubbles (right) and Pemetic Mountain over Eagle Lake

When you've had a chance to look around at the surrounding hills, descend to the junction with the North Bubble Trail, turning left and beginning the walk up the second peak. The route is to the north through more dwarf birch and over ledge with Pemetic and Cadillac Mountains in striking profile to the east and northeast. You shortly pass several cairns and proceed over the creased granite mentioned earlier. Mountain cranberries lie beneath a corridor of young pitch pines and red spruces as you walk on the summit of North Bubble.

From this second peak, a beautiful view of Eagle Lake to the north greets you. Beyond it further to the northeast is the great expanse of Frenchman Bay. Off to the west is the long massif of Penobscot and Sargent Mountains. This more northerly of the two Bubbles is the higher at nearly 900 feet, and from it you can look back over the route you've followed thus far, and also ahead to the route down to the north along the ridge toward Conners Nubble and Eagle Lake.

Head down the open ridge which supports little growth, having been burned over in the great Bar Harbor fires of 1947. Follow the cairns down the ledges, enjoying the continuing views of Cadillac, Acadia's highest mountain, as you proceed northward. A little more than ¾ mile below the north summit you reach a carriage trail. Bear right and east here and walk another ¾ mile downhill into the woods until you reach the Jordan Pond Carry Trail. Turn right here onto this sometimes wet, boggy trail and ascend slowly through beech and hemlock groves to the first trail junction of this hike. At the junction, go left and you'll regain the parking area in a couple of minutes.

Saint Sauveur–Flying Mountain Loop

Distance (round trip): 6 miles
Hiking time: 3 hours
Vertical rise: 1100 feet
Maps: USGS 7½' Southwest Harbor; USGS Acadia National
Park and Vicinity; AMC Map of Mount Desert Island

For fine views over the narrows at the south end of magnificent Somes Sound, the circle over Saint Sauveur and Flying Mountains near Southwest Harbor makes an excellent walk. This route takes the hiker over three low summits in the less-frequented quarter of Mount Desert Island. The walk is both prettily wooded in sections and also barren, ledgy, and open in places, providing a platform that looks to seaward. And, because Saint Sauveur lies in an area off the beaten tourist path, you can walk here with relative privacy even in high summer.

The hike begins at the same spot as the Acadia mountain loop (see Hike 41) on ME 102, 3 miles south of Somesville and 3 miles north of Southwest Harbor. The parking area on 102 is well marked and easy to find directly across from the trailhead. There are some fine outlooks over Echo Lake, too, as you drive south from Somesville.

You enter the woods headed eastward on the Acadia Mountain Trail and follow this path for just a short distance before reaching the Saint Sauveur Trail on your right. Bear right here and begin the straightforward march to the southeast up the northwest flanks of Saint Sauveur.

These are pretty woods, characterized by abundant Scotch pine, gray birch, and other young hardwoods. Crossing a seasonal brook and passing through several clearings, you rise gradually toward the summit with views of Acadia Mountain opening up behind you. One mile from your starting place, you pass the Ledge Trail on your right and continue southeast another ⅓ mile, now out in the open, to the bare, ledgy summit of Saint Sauveur.

The mountain takes its name from the ill-fated French settlement established here by the Jesuits in 1613. The French mission had set out for Bangor but had been blown into Frenchman Bay by inclement weather. After exploring the south coast of the island, the lower reaches of Somes Sound seemed a good place to establish a base, particularly with good water available in nearby Man o' War Brook. However, in just weeks, the colony was discovered by the patrolling English frigate *Treasurer* under command of Samuel Argall.

James I of England claimed Mount Desert's shores during this period, and the mandate of English coasters was to put short shrift to any French attempts to develop permanent settlements here. In

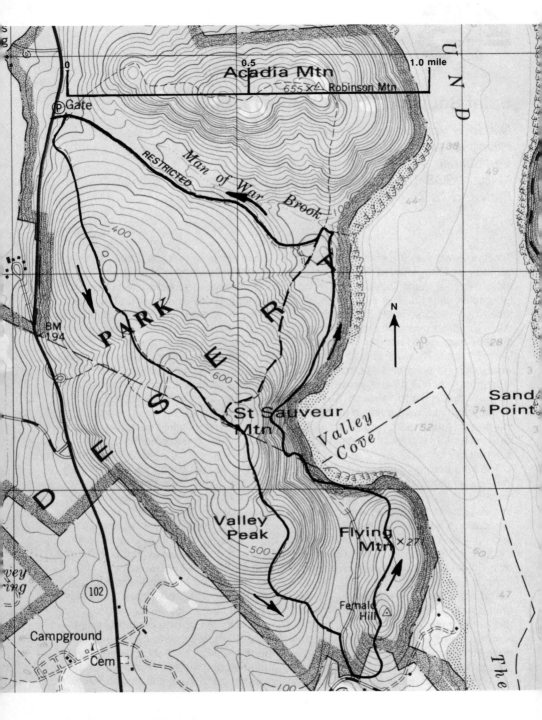

Acadia Mtn

655 X△ Robinson Mtn

0   0.5   1.0 mile

Gate

RESTRICTED

Man of War Brook

P A R K E R S E D E

400

BM 194

600

St Sauveur Mtn

N

Sand Point

Valley Cove

152

Valley Peak

500

Flying Mtn ×271

60

Female Hill △

102

100

Campground

Cem

vey ring

138

49

44

120

28

3

34

47

The

full battle dress, the *Treasurer* bore down on the French ship *Jonas*, moored off Fernald Cove below Flying Mountain. The French were quite unprepared for the arrival of an English 14-gunner, and fled into the woods of Saint Sauveur. Members of the short-lived colony surrendered to the British the next day. A full and colorful description of this and other military and naval actions can be found in Samuel Eliot Morrison's *The Story of Mount Desert Island*, available in many shops in Bar Harbor and Ellsworth.

Saint Sauveur's summit ledges are surrounded by low spruce, so the views are less good here than on the ridge you've just come up and further along in this hike. Proceed off the summit to Eagle Cliffs, a far better outlook, just past a clearing laced with juniper bushes. The panorama of Somes Sound, spreading itself out beneath you, is magnificent, and you'll probably want to rest here a while and enjoy watching the movement of boats up and down the Sound. Valley Cove is the rounded bay immediately to the east.

From Eagle Cliffs, take the left trail at a junction and descend gradually to Valley Peak through juniper and blueberry bushes. Valley Peak is actually an arm of Saint Sauveur Mountain that offers additional opportunities to see the ocean and the Sound as you proceed south-eastward. Moving through cedar and spruce cover, you walk over heavily gouged granite ledge and onto Valley Peak's 520-foot summit.

The trail next pulls around to the west, providing good views of Fernald's Cove and Southwest Harbor. Gnarled oaks and white pines border the path as you descend nearly to sea level. You walk through a cedar bog and over two plank bridges, emerging in minutes on a gravel right-of-way known as Valley Cove Truck Road. Head right on the road for 100 yards, and then bear left on Flying Mountain Trail, which is clearly marked. Making the turn here, you're at the most southerly point on the walk.

The walk takes you uphill again through columns of tall cedars on Flying Mountain's south arm. Very shortly you arrive on the ledgy summit. Valley Peak, Beech, and Mansell Mountains are off to the northwest. The pot shape of Greening Island floats to the southeast off Southwest Harbor. Fernald Cove is directly below you to the south. Although Flying Mountain is the lowest of the three moderate summits in this loop, you have the feeling of being up high here because of the abrupt rise of these hills from the water.

Resuming the hike, you'll bear around to the east looking out over the Narrows. If you happen to hit this spot at low tide, you'll note that Somes Sound is nearly a lake at such moments, given the shallow bar at the Narrows. You now descend fairly steeply for ⅓ mile to Valley Cove. On a warm summer day, you may want to picnic here and have a swim. To get on the beach, leave the trail where it crosses a footbridge near the shore. Valley Cove Spring signs appear momentarily. This *may* be a source of water, but is unpredictable.

Skirting the cove, you proceed through a collection of boulders where polypody fern, rock tripe, and moss grow. Cross a slide and ascend a series of stone steps as you move north of the cove. The sheer bulk of Eagle Cliffs hangs above you to the left on Saint Sauveur. Continuing still northward, cross another slide, which requires caution, and pick up the trail again on its other side. The trail then drops to the water's edge and enters the woods.

After a short walk along the shore of the Sound, you enter a cedar bog and

Fernald Cove and Greening Island from Valley Peak

come to Man o' War Brook. Watch for a woods road on the left, and turn west here. This is the same route back to the highway that one takes when completing the Acadia Mountain loop. From here, walk through a field and you'll reach the end of Robinson Road in a few hundred yards. You then continue to the northwest through groves of cedar and, staying with the trail, reach ME 102 and your car in about ½ mile.

Beech Mountain

Distance (around loop): 3½ miles
Hiking time: 2½ hours
Vertical rise: 700 feet
Maps: USGS 7½' Southwest Harbor; USGS Acadia National
  Park and Vicinity; AMC Map of Mount Desert Island

Beech Mountain is one of a circle of low hills in the remote western quarter of Mount Desert Island and is notable for its unspoiled beauty. Situated on the little-traveled west side of Echo Lake, Beech Mountain is the highest point on a long ridge separating Echo Lake and the much larger Long Pond. A variety of paths winds around the mountain through attractive woods, boulder gardens, and splendid, open ledges. Except for the initial gain in altitude, the trail is not difficult or demanding. Even a beginning hiker will find this an easy and very pleasant walk.

To reach the mountain, follow ME 3 south and east from Ellsworth to its junction with ME 102 and 198 just beyond the Thompson Island Information Center as you enter Mount Desert Island. Bear right and follow ME 102 to Somesville. From the center of this little village, bear right ⅓ mile past Higgins Market and continue on 102 as it heads west. In less than ¼ mile you bear left onto Beech Hill Road. The road runs south along a high ridge, gradually leaves the houses behind, and rolls toward Beech Mountain. Pretty, open fields, grown thick with low-bush blueberries, yield fine views to Beech

and to Bernard and Mansell Mountains to the southwest and to other ranges on the island off to the east.

Beech Hill Road ends abruptly at a parking lot just over 3 miles from its junction with 102. Park to the right under the cliffs. Take the trail that leaves the northwest corner of the parking area. This trail moves upward to the west for several hundred yards before coming to a trail junction. Keep to the left at the junction and take the higher of two trails to the summit. On this route, you shortly move onto open ledge with excellent outlooks back to the north over Echo Lake and to Somesville with its prominent white church steeple. Good views across Somes Sound to Norumbega and Penobscot Mountains are found here too. In less than ½ mile from the parking lot, you arrive at the convergence of the two trails at the observation tower on Beech's 839-foot summit.

Beech's summit plateau, overgrown with sheep laurel, provides 360-degree views including those to the south toward Greening Island, the Cranberry Isles, and the Atlantic. Mansell and Bernard Mountains loom to the southwest across the southern neck of Long Pond. The pond, a beautiful, slim

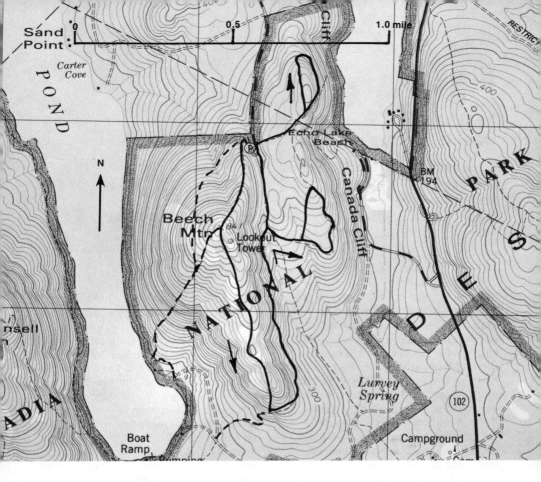

expanse of water running north and south, is the largest landlocked body of water on Mount Desert.

To continue beyond the summit, take the South Ridge Trail toward the ocean, descending a granite ridge dotted with lichen. The route is alternately in the open and in the woods. You are as likely as not to see deer tracks along here. British soldiers—tiny, red-capped lichens—cranberries, gray-green reindeer lichen, and heather grow among the rocks. Reaching a set of stone steps, you take a sharp left downhill. The open ledges now give way to shady bowers of spruce. A series of switchbacks descends through mossy cascades and thick groves of birch and beech, bringing you to a junction with a side trail that runs to Long Pond. Heading away from the pond, instead bear left onto the Valley Trail. Walk due north on the Valley Trail, passing through varied growth and past a jumble of granite slabs stacked here long ago by glacial movement. This ancient stonework is now covered with polypody fern and a foliose lichen known as rock tripe.

From where you made the turn onto the Valley Trail to the parking area is just under 1 mile. Approximately ⅔ mile along this path, you come to the Canada Cliffs Loop Trail on your right. Turn right and east here at the sign, cross a boggy area, climb a brief rise, and then walk down through a cedar bog on a series of plank bridges. This trail shortly forks, each side being the "leg" of a loop over the cliffs. Keep right and you'll soon be on the ledges with fine views east to Saint Sauveur Mountian. The other leg of the trail comes in about 50 yards from the summit. Make a mental note of this spot, as you'll return on the other leg on your way back to the Valley Trail. A walk of a few more yards brings you to the high point on these dramatic, open cliffs with excellent outlooks to Echo Lake and the northeast. Picking up the other leg of the loop, proceed briefly west to the Valley Trail, and then turn northward or right toward your starting place. It is only 5 to 10 minutes' walk to the parking area.

If, when you reach the parking lot, you've still some energy left, another short loop runs off to the northeast over Beech Cliff. Look for the sign that indicates this loop across the road opposite the northeast corner of the parking lot. Keep left just past the sign and make the short walk (about ⅓ mile) through groves of spruce and cedar eastward to Beech Cliff over Echo Lake. The views over Echo Lake are even better than those you experienced on Canada Cliffs. The granite here bears the familiar scouring of glacial activity so common on the summits of Mount Desert.

After passing over the top point of this cliff, you bear around to the south on a lower trail, gradually pulling west and rejoining the short leg to the parking lot. On this lower, return loop, you come around again to the fork where you stayed left on the way in. A third trail here makes a rise over a hill and then descends gradually through a series of ladders and switchbacks to Echo Lake. The walk down this third trail to the water is about a ¾-mile round trip and may be worth the extra effort on a hot day. (This third trail to the water is not included in the time and distance estimates at the top of this hike description.)

Valley Trail below Beech Mountain

Mansell and Bernard Mountain Loop

Distance (round trip): 5 miles
Hiking time: 4 hours
Vertical rise: 1500 feet
Maps: USGS Acadia National Park and Vicinity; AMC Map of
  Mount Desert Island

Overlooking Blue Hill Bay and the islands southwest of Mount Desert, the bulky massif known as Western Mountain dominates the westerly precincts of Acadia National Park. Western Mountain, a name not much used anymore, is actually comprised of two summits, Mansell Mountain on the east and Bernard Mountain to the west. The two are divided by a north-south cleft called Great Notch. An interesting loop over these two peaks provides 5 miles of challenging hiking on the remote fringes of Acadia. As Western Mountain is criss-crossed by a whole network of trails leading in various directions, the hiker should carry a compass, a local map, and this trail description to avoid making a wrong turn.

This hike begins at the pumping station at the south end of Long Pond. This site is reached by driving south from the junction of ME 198 and ME 102 in Somesville. Take ME 102 toward Southwest Harbor and turn right on Seal Cove Road just under 6 miles from the junction in Somesville. Once on Seal Cove Road, drive ½ mile to a fork where you bear right onto Long Pond Road. Continue west here for 1¼ miles and park by the pumping station.

Look for a trail marker where the route departs to the northwest along the shore of Long Pond. Walking just a few yards, you come upon a second sign that points left. Don't turn here, but make a mental note. You will return to the road on this other path. Staying with the shore of the pond, you walk along with Beech Mountain over to the right and Mansell Mountain above to your left. You move through cedar groves rich with club moss here.

In just ¼ mile, you bear left and begin to climb on the Perpendicular Trail. That name should be enough to indicate a fairly steep rise, but the route is not difficult. Follow this path upward over stone steps and through more cedar and young spruce, coming shortly to a rock slide. A series of stone steps and iron rungs takes you up the slide. Good views of Beech and Acadia Mountains open up behind you to the east as you climb. Views of the Atlantic over South-west Harbor can be seen around to the southeast. Rock tripe, reindeer lichen, and polypody fern grow on the slide. Beyond the slide, waxy, white shoots of Indian pipe prosper in the shady undergrowth.

The trail now turns to the right,

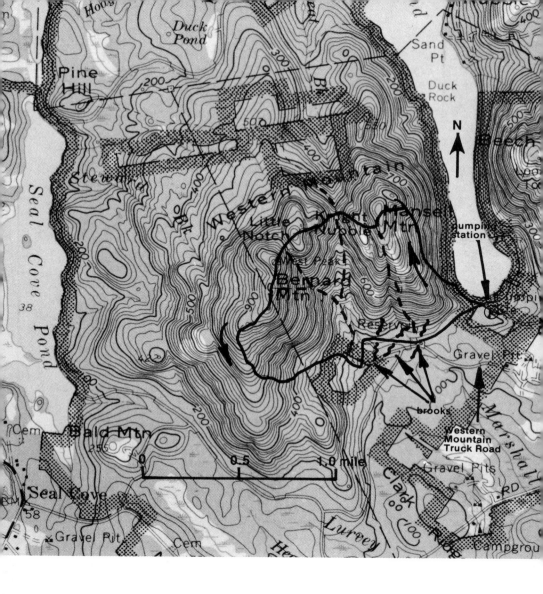

hugging a long ridge of granite topped with young cedars. Soon you level off in a birch grove, and then ascend again up another set of stone steps and past a seasonal brook. The trail reaches a stream bed, pulls left, and then follows a series of cairns and red markers to a junction with an outlook to your right.

Here you can see eastward toward Greening Island and Sutton Island.

Head west into the trees from the junction, staying with the cairns and red markers toward Mansell's summit. There is more uphill work here over a series of boulders surrounded by red spruce. In minutes, you'll arrive on Mansell's 949-

foot wooded summit. The trail continues through some blowdown and another grove of darker, weathered red spruce. Shortly, another trail junction is reached with views ahead to Knight Nubble and Bernard Mountain. Proceed in their direction, following the cairns and red markers.

Your climbing labors now yield to a steep scramble down into Great Notch, dipping downward through stands of spruce and sheep laurel. At a trail junction, turn southwest toward Great Notch. You walk over a granite ridge, and then bear to the right abruptly and into dense red spruce in the heart of the Notch. You'll come upon a clearing momentarily where there are log benches and a trail sign. Here you turn uphill on the Knight Nubble Trail. A march of less than ¼ mile brings you to some stone steps, and, just beyond, the 930-foot high point. This summit is wooded, too, but a short side trail just before you reach the top provides a good view to the southeast.

From here, you proceed southwest-ward, dipping into Little Notch, and climbing again in ¼ mile to the summit of Bernard Mountain. The most dramatic sights of this walk are all around you here. The northeast side of Bernard Mountain is heavily littered with blow-down through which young spruce is beginning to grow again. Views of 180 degrees range from Blue Hill off to the west and over Beech Mountain to the major summits in the center of the Island. (You are not actually on the true summit of Bernard Mountain here. It lies 100 yards further back into the woods in a clearing.)

The final segment of the loop requires that you head downhill through some old, dense spruce growth toward the Western Mountain Truck Road. The trail runs southwest and then pulls around to the southeast. At a trail junction, you bear right on the South Face Trail and descend through spindly red spruce and brilliant mossy ground cover. Blueberry bushes, cranberries, and sheep laurel grow along the route. Views south to Swan's Island, Bass Harbor, and west to Deer Isle open up here from time to time. Two streams are crossed as the trail pulls more easterly and soft-woods yield to beech. As you cross a third stream, turn to the right and you'll come in just a few steps to Western Mountain Truck Road.

Once on the truck road, continue east for 30 yards, and then fork left into the woods. In just ¹⁄₁₀ mile you'll come to a small stone reservoir with a spillway. Facing the reservoir, you head right and east uphill on the Gilley Trail. Almost at once you come to another junction where you bear right and walk less than ¼ mile to Gilley Field. (A copy of the AMC Map of Mount Desert Island is very useful to maintain your bearings in this confusing section of tangled pathways.) Coming shortly to a turnaround on a dirt road, you follow the signs to Long (Great) Pond. The walk now is less than ½ mile through pretty woods grown up in beech, maple, birch, and spruce. The trail emerges at the junction mentioned at the start of this walk. Just bear right and you'll arrive at the pumping station where you parked.

Eastern Maine—the "Air Line" and the Eastern Maine Coast

Great Pond Mountain

Distance (round trip): 4¼ miles
Hiking time: 2½ hours
Vertical rise: 650 feet
Map: USGS 15' Orland

Great Pond Mountain, sometimes referred to as "Great Hill," tends to be a locals' mountain, the source of a perfect hike never overrun by the hoards who race by hell-bent for the more famous hills of Mount Desert to the east. Largely undiscovered, well hidden back in the woods to the north of US 1 in Orland, Great Pond Mountain provides a relaxed, beautiful walk in quiet surroundings reminiscent of a Maine less traveled. The route rewards the hiker with exceptional views without much vertical scrambling, and it's easy enough to bring youngsters along without complaint. In short, you'll find this a great family hike with only positive surprises.

The mountain is approached from US 1 on a side road which leaves the main highway at a point 1½ miles east of the junction of US 1 and ME 15 in Orland (6 miles east of the center of Bucksport). Turn north onto the side road, signed Craig Brook National Fish Hatchery, and follow this road, which is first paved and then gravel, westward to the hatchery grounds. Park by the visitors' center.

If this is a first visit, you may wish to spend some time exploring the Craig Brook Hatchery grounds before setting out. You are on the site of America's oldest salmon hatchery, established in 1871. The hatchery raceways and display pool are visible on the hillside which drops toward Alamoosook Lake. The visitors' center provides interesting displays and information on the propagation and research done at this facility, which began with the work of Dr. Charles Atkins in the late 1860s.

The trail to Great Pond Mountain leaves the notice board by the visitors' center and runs west for a moment along the road, making an immediate turn around some buildings to the right and north. Follow this pleasant, shady, gravel road as it meanders northward toward 200-acre Craig Pond. In about a half mile, you pass a grassy turnout to the right where a nature trail makes a 1-mile scenic loop through the Craig Brook area. Continuing northward, you stay on the main gravel road, passing several roads or paths which drift off into the woods. Just over a mile from your starting point and just before you reach the Craig Pond gate, look for a very rough gravel road which forks to the left. Here you begin the uphill tramp to the ledgy summit of Great Pond Mountain. Head up the gravel side road; it's scoured and even, and becomes a

The trail on Great Pond Mountain

streambed in wet weather. You'll pass a message box, placed by the Great Pond Mountain Conservation Trust, on a tree to your right. Follow the road west and northwestward. Wild raspberries, goldenrod, and dense brush border the road. This land appears to have been logged over about a decade or so ago. You pass a side road to your left, and continue uphill briskly through young beech and ash.

The road rises quickly, and scattered hemlocks appear. Sections of fractured and weathered granodioritic rock lie in the roadbed. As you proceed, this rock becomes fully exposed, giving the road an almost paved look. The route pulls around to the right and north by a small cairn, passing a grassy road that departs to the left. Coniferous trees begin to grow in greater density here, with white pine, red spruce, and balsam evident. The air carries their pleasing fragrance.

Running through a clearing, the road reenters a wooded area and, climbing gradually, pulls around toward the east and northeast. The land to the west begins to drop away, and you have a sense of gaining altitude. The road crosses bands of ledge, returning here and there to gravel and narrowing to a path in places. The exposed ledge gives a hint of its formation in a molten state, millions of years ago, and seems to flow downward in frozen waves. You can also see how thin the topsoil is here over the great, stone underlayment, yet grasses and trees manage to hold on.

The road divides briefly around a little island of trees at a tall hemlock. Going east and northeast, you pass a grove of older hemlock; beech and white birch appear. Soon you walk into a more open area, where the route turns northward. White oak and pine border a grassy verge. Some views over Alamoosook

Lake begin to open to the south. Ground blueberries grow plentifully to the left of the trail.

The summit ledges become visible higher up and to the north. Dotted with lichen-crusted rock, this spot has a pleasant, open feel to it. Birch, spruce, balsam, and more oak lie along the way. Haircap and sphagnum mosses are visible. Keep your eyes open, too, for a little side trail on the left through stands of evergreens. A few steps off the main route here will bring you to good early views to the southwest and west. If you cross the main trail and walk eastward, there are also fine views to the east and southeast. You can, in fact, easily see all the way to the Atlantic on a clear day.

At the top of this long, open rise the trail turns sharply left and then right again, rising further through dense evergreens. It is interesting to see how closely the climatic zones are layered on this little mountain. In this colder elevation, you have left the deciduous growth mostly behind. You shortly pass a road that comes in on the left. (Remember this point, and remember to bear *left* at this junction on your descent.) A series of open, ledgy clearings alternates with sections where spruce and hemlock crowd the path. Bunchberries, scattered ferns, white pines, and birches border the way.

You now climb the final rise to the summit ledges. The route turns abruptly right, then left, arriving on the more-or-less flat and open summit, a great pancake of granitic ledge. (The true summit, only slightly higher and more wooded, is through the grove of evergreens to the north.) Before you are 180-degree outlooks over some of Maine's most handsome coastal terrain. The numerous peaks of Mount Desert lie to the east, south of prominent Schoodic Mountain. The distinctive, conelike lump

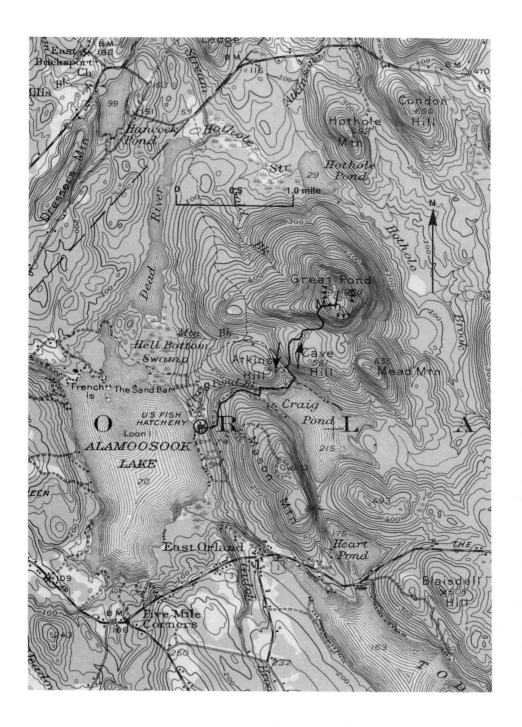

of Blue Hill is to the southeast. Mount Waldo rises around to the west on the other side of Bucksport. Branch, Green, and Graham lakes are in the valleys to eastward. Almost anywhere on these rangy ledges makes a good picnic spot, and you aren't likely to be disturbed by many visitors even at the height of the summer season.

Although Great Pond Mountain is a pleasant climb year-round, it's superb in foliage season, both for its broad views over much forestland, and also for the colorful, mixed vegetation along its own path. The experienced snowshoer or hiker with crampons will find it an excellent and challenging winter walk, too.

To regain your starting point, carefully retrace your steps down the mountain and southward on the access road, being careful not to leave the main route on any of the numerous side roads and trails which head off in various directions.

Peaked Mountain (Chick Hill)

Distance (round trip): 2½ miles
Hiking time: 1½ hours
Vertical rise: 800 feet
Map: USGS 15' Great Pond

Peaked Mountain, known locally as Chick Hill, is found in the center of Hancock County, about 18 miles east of Bangor on the Air Line (ME 9) between Clifton and Amherst. This low mountain with two open, ledgy summits offers a striking profile to travelers on ME 9, particularly those approaching from the west. An abandoned, 40-foot fire tower on the higher of the two summits affords an exceptional vantage point over what is largely wild, unspoiled country.

The mountain can be reached by driving east from Bangor on ME 9 and looking left for the access road 12.5 miles east of the junction of ME 9 and ME 178 in Eddington. If you arrive from the east, turn right on the access road 3.5 miles west of the junction of ME 9 and ME 180 in Clifton. This side road is known as Chick Hill Road, but the sign is not right on ME 9, but up the side road about 100 feet, mounted high on a utility pole. This turn is easily located by watching for a "Fire Road 31" sign facing west on ME 9.

Turning north on Chick Hill Road, you shortly run out of pavement. Continue around the bend and uphill to the right on a gravel surface past several houses and mobile homes. You will be able to see the mountain on your right. In barely 0.5 mile, the road forks. Park off the right-of-way here.

The trail, an old carriage road which used to be a link in the Air Line many years ago, has grown over with tall grass and is sheltered by dense mixed growth. Walk up this steep woods road to the northeast, passing the old warden's cabin site in about ¼ mile. A spring-fed brook here is the last water on this hike. Jack-in-the-pulpits, fireweed, and several varieties of fern bloom alongside the trail here in spring and summer.

Soon you pass a grassy tote road on your right and fork to the left at ½ mile from where you parked. The trail levels off some just beyond this section, and then bears right off the old road you've been following and onto a smaller woods road designated by old ax blazes. Here and there the downed line of the warden's telephone may be seen. You next climb gradually through stands of maple, young oak, and striped maple.

The trail begins a sharp rise at just under 1 mile. As you begin this steeper ascent, you will see Little Peaked Mountain to your right. It is the westernmost of the three summits that are lumped together as "Chick Hill" by

Peaked Mountain from the "Air Line"

Eastern Maine–the "Air Line" and the Eastern Maine Coast

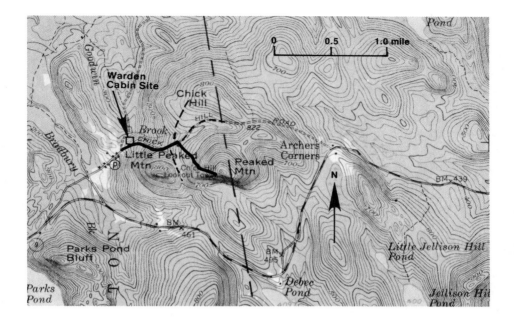

local people. This summit is trailless, but it can be climbed by bushwhacking southwest from the col between it and Peaked Mountain, your destination. The best views lie ahead on the higher summit, however.

You continue southeastward now on the steep rise to Peaked Mountain (referred to locally as "Big Chick"), shortly arriving on the open ledges marked by several cairns. Your route here runs over coarse granite. The top of Little Peaked Mountain becomes visible at your back. The eroded rock path soon brings you to the summit of Peaked Mountain and the disused warden's tower. Scattered blueberry patches dot the summit.

The 1160-foot summit and the tower provide 360-degree views over Hancock County and east into Washington County. Chemo Pond and the Penobscot River are to your west over Little Peaked.

Far to the northwest you may see Katahdin if the weather is clear. Chick Hill, whose name has been generalized to all three summits, is the small knob to the immediate north. Saddleback Mountain, Fletcher Bluff, and Bald Mountain are prominent peaks to the northeast in Amherst. Lead Mountain (see Hike 50) lies far off to the east. Bradbury Brook divides a marsh to the southeast across the road. Some of the major summits of Acadia National Park on Mount Desert Island show up to the south if hazy skies don't obscure them. Debec Pond and Hopkins Pond rest immediately below to the south.

The walk back to your car retraces the route of the ascent. You may want to make the side trip to Little Peaked Mountain on your way down. Use caution on the exposed, ledgy areas of both mountains.

Lead Mountain

Distance (round trip): 5½ miles
Hiking time: 3 hours
Vertical rise: 1150 feet
Map: USGS 15' Lead Mountain

Lead Mountain, sometimes known as Humpback, lies about 40 miles east of Bangor and about 45 miles west of Calais on the Air Line (ME 9) in the middle of nowhere. That, indeed, is one of the attractions of this and other hills in the area: few people, little or no development, and lots of deep woods and wildlife. The mountain rises just to the west of the Hancock-Washington County line over the Narraguagas River. Although lumbering has had some effect on the mountain in recent years, Lead Mountain is still a good walk with fine views of this much underrated corner of Maine.

To reach the trailhead, drive east from Bangor on ME 9. You shortly pass through the town of Eddington. The mountain road is 37.5 miles east of the junction of 9 and ME 178 here. If you approach from the south on ME 180 from the Ellsworth area, the mountain road is 28.5 miles east of the junction of 180 and ME 9 in Clifton. Watch for a Maine Forest Service sign a short drive east of the county line and just west of the Narraguagas River bridge. There are good views of the mountain as you approach from east or west, with the best perhaps being from a high hill that

ME 9 traverses immediately east of the Narraguagas.

Turn north into the forest service driveway and park on your left in a gravel field opposite the warden's house. A trail departs the northwest corner of this lot along an abandoned tote road now marked for snowmobile use in winter. Almost at once, you come to a fork in the road; keep right through a grove of pines. In less than 100 yards, this road intersects with a newer, gravel road which you will follow for most of this hike.

Turn left and northwest on the gravel road, keeping your eyes and ears peeled for infrequent lumber truck activity. You pass now through three fairly distinct timber staging areas. The sides of the road are buried in old slash, and you can spot where tote roads came in from other areas to these clearings. Continuing to the west and northwest, you quickly march up a rise as the road bears more around to the right. Beyond the clearings, spruce, hemlock, and maple growth lines the right-of-way. Blueberries, blackberries, and bracken fern are found, too.

You next follow the road as it meanders gradually to the northwest, passing

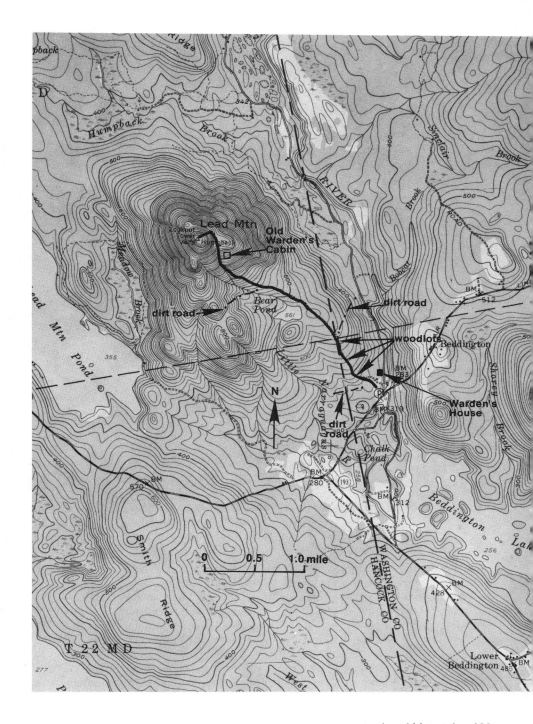

Lead Mtn

Old Warden's Cabin

Lookout Tower

Humpback

Humpback Brook

Bear Pond

dirt road

dirt road

woodlots

Beddington

Warden's House

dirt road

Chalk Pond

N

Smith Ridge

T 22 MD

Meadow Brook

Mtn Pond

RIVER

Sinclair Brook

Brook

Bobcat

Brook

Sharry Brook

Beddington Lake

WASHINGTON CO
HANCOCK CO

Lower Beddington

0   0.5   1.0 mile

BM 283

BM 319

BM 312

BM 280

193

BM 428

BM 485

Lead Mountain Pond from Lead Mountain

many side roads and turnouts now piled high with stumpage. Approximately ½ mile from where you began, you will see tiny Bear Pond through the trees to your left not far in from the road. Take a moment to push your way through the balsam and black spruce here to get a look at the pond. If the time of day is right and you've been quiet enough, you may see deer or moose. The elevation of the pond is 561 feet.

The road rises very gradually to the northwest and reaches a clearing and a gate. A small house trailer has been parked here temporarily by researchers probing the acid rain problem and its effects on Maine woodlands. Don't be put off by the "No Trespassing" signs.

It's okay to walk, but not drive, beyond this point. The gate is about 1 mile from the start.

Beyond the gate, the road, narrower now, rises more steeply toward the humpback through mixed growth for another mile and dwindles to a path as you climb more briskly up the southeast side of the mountain. The old warden's cabin, boarded up and forlorn, is passed in a col below the summit. A clearing dotted with raspberry bushes is soon reached, and you continue up to the west, landing on the flat, open summit.

Lead Mountain once supported a fire tower and observer, but the tower and those who manned it are long gone. A small communications mast has since been erected on the summit. Scrub growth makes it pretty hard to see anything from this spot, but if you walk south about 200 yards to the ledges, the views south and west are rewarding. Pick some of the low-bush blueberries that grow here in abundance in late July and early August, and enjoy your lunch. Upper, Middle, and Lower Lead Mountain Ponds lie off to the southwest and west. You can also see Schoodic Mountain over to the south above Frenchman Bay, accompanied by Tunk, Caribou, and Black Mountains. Far to the west nearer Bangor is Peaked Mountain, or Chick Hill as it is sometimes known (see Hike 49). If you're willing to go over the summit and climb a tree, you may get some good views up into Washington County as well.

In hiking Lead Mountain, remember that the area is subject to occasional logging activity by the paper company that owns it. The gravel road you walked may have been extended to obliterate the trail, or additional side roads may have been constructed by the time you make this walk. Watch for any signs of the trail departing the road at points other than those described here. Carry a compass and keep in mind that the route to the summit is generally in a northwesterly direction, southeasterly in the return. Bring food and water in your pack. And, if you descend at dusk, don't be surprised to see a family of deer looking back at you as they cross the road. Despite the presence of the gravel right-of-way, this is still wild country.

Books from The Countryman Press
and Backcountry Publications

The Countryman Press and Backcountry Publications, long known for fine books on travel and outdoor recreation, offer a range of practical and readable manuals.

Hiking Series:

Fifty Hikes in the Adirondacks, $13.00
Fifty Hikes in Central New York, $13.00
Fifty Hikes in Central Pennsylvania, $13.00
Fifty Hikes in Connecticut, $12.00
Fifty Hikes in Eastern Pennsylvania, $12.00
Fifty Hikes in the Hudson Valley, $14.00
Fifty Hikes in Lower Michigan, $13.00
Fifty Hikes In Massachusetts, $13.00
Fifty Hikes in New Jersey, $13.00
Fifty Hikes in Northern Maine, $12.00
Fifty Hikes in Northern Virginia, $13.00
Fifty Hikes in Ohio, $13.00
Fifty Hikes in Southern Maine, $12.00
Fifty Hikes in Vermont, $12.00
Fifty Hikes in Western New York, $13.00
Fifty Hikes in Western Pennsylvania, $12.00
Fifty Hikes in the White Mountains, $14.00
Fifty More Hikes in New Hampshire, $14.00

Walks & Rambles Series:

Walks & Rambles in Dutchess and Putnam Counties, $11.00
Walks & Rambles in Rhode Island, Second Edition, $11.00
More Walks & Rambles in Rhode Island, $11.00
Walks and Rambles in Westchester & Fairfield Counties, Second Edition, $11.00
Walks & Rambles in the Upper Connecticut River Valley, $10.00
Walks & Rambles on Cape Cod and the Islands, $11.00
Walks & Rambles on the Delmarva Peninsula, $11.00

We offer many more books on hiking, walking, fishing, and canoeing plus books on travel, nature, and many other subjects.

Our books are available through bookstores, or they may be ordered directly from the publisher. For shipping and handling costs, to order, or for a complete catalog, please contact: The Countryman Press, Inc., P.O. Box 175AP, Woodstock, VT 05091, or call our toll-free number, (800) 245-4151. Prices and availability are subject to change.